Letters To My Teenage Self

NICOLE BATEMAN, KASEY ALICE, HOLLY FOSTER, ELOISE GROBBELAAR, FAYE HANCOCK, EMILY JOLLIFFE, KALINI KENT, CHARLOTTE LEWINGTON, EVA OLAVE MARTINEZ, JANE MILLER, EMMA RIMMER, CASSIE SWIFT, ENJOYMASUELA TJORN

Contents

Foreword

By Meggan Larson

I am no stranger to difficulties during my teen years. Adopted as a baby, I longed to know who I belonged to and why I was given away by the very people who were supposed to love me unconditionally. I struggled with the fear of rejection so badly that I couldn't physically look people in the eye until my twenties.

I wish that I had read a book like *Letters To My Teenage Self* back then. What a difference it might have made in my life to know that I wasn't alone. To know that there were others who had struggled the same way I had but had overcome.

This book is full of authentic and moving stories of women who overcame hardships and are reaching back to give a helping hand to other teens—the way they wished they had been supported It's a beautiful collection of emotional and raw stories that will hopefully reach many teens who need to know that they'll get through this and that they'll be okay. The world needs more books like this one.

xo Meggan Larson – Winner of the Indie Reader Discovery Award—Coming Of Age category for her novel "Adopted".

CHAPTER ONE

To the teen who doesn't feel good enough

BY NICOLE BATEMAN

TO THE TEEN WHO doesn't feel good enough...

Sitting in my room... alone... my brain in overdrive... I was weighing up this massive decision. I didn't want to fail. I didn't want to be seen as a failure. But being a doctor... that's such a great achievement... that's what I should be. I mean, I'm good at science, and I want to help people... so that's the route I should go down...

BUT it wasn't what I expected.

BUT it wasn't what I wanted.

I was spending hours doing something that I wasn't passionate about, not wanting to disappoint others. If I'm a doctor, then everyone will be so proud of me. Maybe when I graduate, when I achieve that accolade, maybe then I would finally feel good enough?

The decision to leave medical school was a huge turning point – a painful learning curve, a taste of failure, but looking back... one I would not change.

Thinking back to my early teenage years, I was often found in my room singing at the top of my voice to all the classic tunes. One I often sang on repeat had a line that said: 'Why is everything so confusing? Maybe I'm just out of my mind...' Sometimes it feels like that, doesn't it!? So much confusion. So many decisions. Believing that if you make the wrong decision now, then you are doomed to fail.

Every decision does have a ripple effect on your life, but you are not doomed to fail. A stone dropped in a pond sends ripples in all directions, not just one. The choices we make do impact our lives; the skill is to adapt, learn new things, and then, we can change our path for the better.

It's hard at school sometimes, isn't it? Trying to make decisions when you're eleven, twelve, thirteen. Trying to think about what you want to be when you're older. What you want to do. There's so much pressure to know what you want to do. The 'older you' has seen that pressure and anxiety in her own students (yes... you actually become a teacher... not a doctor... but that's only part of your journey!)

You've seen teens being torn between what they actually enjoy and find interesting and expectations of what society sees as 'successful' and a well thought out career path. What if everyone chose what they enjoyed, what they were passionate about? What if everyone did that? Wouldn't the world be such a better place!

You got very competitive at school, even in primary school. You had a lovely group of friends who were all very high achieving, and you always wanted to be the best. Even at a young age, you tied part of your identity to the grades you achieved.

At secondary school, you wanted to be getting all those A*s at GCSE (9s these days). And you were surrounded by some very clever people, too. You wanted to be the best! I remember that childlike competitiveness of comparing who got the best marks in tests and who got to the extension questions in class.

The pressure intensified when you went to secondary school. It was a high-achieving private school, and you got in on a scholarship - an academic scholarship no less. So the pressure was there right from the start. There was a need to prove that you were worth that scholarship and that you would fulfil the expectation. Your parents have always encouraged you and championed you. They always wanted the best for you so that you could have loads of opportunities for later in life.

You had (and still have) high expectations of yourself – now that is both a good and a bad thing. It has given you a fierce determination and drive to not give up when things are tough, but it has also led to feelings of self-doubt. Feelings of not being good enough often creep in if you do not reach the high bar you set for yourself. You wanted to achieve everything you could and had the deep desire to make everyone proud.

You got the results you wanted, and when you got those grades, you felt that sense of pride. You got the praise. You got the recognition, and that helped you feel good. But what I've learnt since then is that if it's the praise that drives you, then any criticism can really hurt you and make you feel worthless.

If you find your identity in the opinions of others, or the grades on the paper, then you will never feel like you are enough. That is a lesson you will learn the hard way as you step out of med school, as you step out of teaching, as you start up your own business. If you constantly compare yourself to others or even compare yourself to your own extremely high standards, you will never be enough. You may be thinking, "Great, thanks for the encouragement," but the only way that you will feel enough is by separating your actual worth from your perception of what others think of you. FACT.

Growing up, you were quite shy and not very confident. People who know me now might think, "What?!" You've always been stubborn. Your stubbornness plays out in a couple of ways in later life... one being that you stand up for what you believe in (something that has been ingrained in you from your parents and grandparents). You always wanted to look out for those on the fringes of society; therefore, you were never part of the 'in-crowd.' You got bullied because of your 'rabbit' teeth. And that hurt you.

I wanted to feel accepted and validated but often looked to external sources rather than focusing on being enough just because I am me. Looking back, I can see that I sought validation through things such as boyfriends and my results. I was not secure in my identity, but being stubborn meant that it has taken me a long time to get to the point of realisation and to change what or whom I find my identity in!

You had never really experienced failure until you were 17. You took your driving test, and you failed. That was the first time that you didn't pass something. That was a shock. You didn't really know how to respond. You over-analysed every turn and mistake you made. Back then, you found your worth and identity in being a 'high achiever,' in being 'clever,' in being the person who 'doesn't fail.' That identity vanished at that moment. Failure was such a different feeling.

You are an interesting dichotomy of a people pleaser who doesn't want to disappoint anyone and also someone who is not afraid to stand up for what you believe in.

I remember standing in the middle of a circle with my friends all around, trying to persuade me to smoke weed. I stood my ground and never did. On the outside, I stayed strong, but internally, I took the taunts to heart.

Sometimes, you try to be strong for others and support them when actually, on the inside, you long for that support too. Sometimes, your strong-willed nature meant that you lost friends... and when you lost friends after sharing your opinions, that just confirmed the feeling of not being 'good enough.' You were left thinking that if you let your opinions out, then you would be rejected. As humans, we long to be accepted, and so rejection can feel like a knife through the soul. Our brains are programmed to keep us safe, so, therefore, we retreat into our shells.

When you hear comments that confirm your common internal thoughts, you often take them to heart. Even a comment said in jest can be over-analysed and remembered years on... 'Oh, you only just got an A in chemistry.' (Back then, an A was the highest grade you could get in your A Levels).

I was left thinking that even though I got the highest that I could, it wasn't enough. If you are in a state of worry or not feeling enough as you are reading this right now, you may have thoughts racing constantly through your brain. These common internal thoughts you have about yourself – often your 'go to' when you are feeling stressed - are called default thoughts. We all have them, and we must work intentionally to reframe them if our default thoughts are negative.

Try challenging them – why aren't you good enough? What's the evidence for that? And who defines what 'good enough' actually is anyway? There's this pressure we put on ourselves to be perfect. We compare our lives with other people and try to be a certain way just because society tells us that it is what you should do, but it doesn't make sense. Why can't we just focus on finding our joy?

Being happy takes priority over winning any competition or achieving an impressive result at school. You are a whole person, and exam results or things that you have achieved are only one pieces of the puzzle – there's a whole lot more to discover.

So if you're not feeling good enough, if you're feeling beaten down by the pressure and the expectations of society or school, or parents, or friends, or yourself, then know that you have many skills and talents. Yes, maybe your skills and talents don't fit the social norms, but ask yourself this – do others get to define you? No, they don't.

For me, a defining moment was when I realised that my identity is not found in boyfriends, popularity, and results but that my identity is found in Jesus. Therefore, I should not care about comparing myself to others. Jesus loves me for who I am. I am unique, and he wants me to let my light shine. I am defined by my identity as a child of God.

Now, you may not believe in God, but either way, don't let your identity be defined by others. Work on what YOU are passionate about. Delve deep and think about what makes you happy. Start with something simple like writing down a list of what you like and don't like.

You can be that change that you want to see in the world. And that is why I'm writing this letter. I'm writing to encourage YOU to be the change that you want to see in your world. If we all do little things, take little steps in a positive direction, then we can be the ripple effect for positive change. If each one of us stands up and shares that we are not defined by our results and not defined by other people, then we can positively change the curvature of society.

We are often searching for a sense of belonging within society, and sometimes, we dim our lights to 'fit in.' I want you to know that what you have to offer the world is so valuable. I want you to shine your light brightly and let the world see you. It's hard if one of your default thoughts is that 'you are not good enough.' It is a thought I continue to tackle and reframe each day. You can't just flick a switch and wake up one day and never have those thoughts again, BUT with practice, bit by bit, you can challenge your default thought, change that thought, and choose to actually believe, 'I'm enough.' You don't need to be anyone else other than yourself... the world needs you!

Sitting in that room... alone... weighing up the big decision of whether to quit medical school and hearing that voice in your head saying, 'everyone will be disappointed in you if you quit.' You need to know that that voice isn't true.

The people who care about you are not disappointed in you; they love you and, therefore, want the best for you – you as a whole person. Unfortunately, sometimes that nagging voice in your head is very convincing! Not everything you think is true. Learn to challenge your thoughts, reframe them, and change the negative thought to a positive – because you definitely have the ability to do that! Positive thoughts will have a positive impact on your feelings, actions, and results.

A simple exercise I want you to try out is that when any negative thoughts come into your head, I want you to challenge them. I want you to think, "What is the basis of this thought? What are the facts? What is evidence against this thought?" Then, I want you to reframe the thought based on facts and evidence – choose to accept the new positive thought – that you are, in fact, good enough.

You, reading this letter, you may not feel like you are in the right place; you may not be feeling good enough. I want you to stop and pause; I want you to look back and see how far you have come, how every choice has rippled through in a positive way, and I want you to appreciate every little step. There are so many different opportunities and ways you can make a difference in life, but first, you need to accept yourself, find your identity, and then, you will be able to live as your full authentic self. And do me a favour … tell that nagging voice in your head to shut up, and tell yourself that YOU ARE VALUABLE, and you ARE, in fact, MORE THAN enough!!

Love, Nicole

P.S. If you are into good singalong sessions like me, then go and pop on Defying Gravity! Don't accept those limits, and don't let others bring you down!

About Author

NICOLE BATEMAN

Nicole is a mum of two, experienced teacher, and creator of "A Box Full of Joy." She is passionate about supporting, encouraging, and empowering young people. Whilst teaching during the pandemic, she noticed an increase in anxiety in her students and widespread low self-esteem. Therefore, she started creating resources help young people to process their worries, communicate their feelings, and deal with overwhelm.

Her stationery, coaching, letterbox gifts, and workshops enable anxious young people to become more resilient, confident, and calm. She wants to encourage teens to be the change they want to see In the world and equip parents with tools to support their teens to thrive.

Nicole brought together authors from around the world to write Letters to my Teenage Self to help teens feel seen in their struggles and give them hope for the future. She wants you, the reader, to know that what you have to offer the world is so valuable.

Take a look at her website: www.aboxfullofjoyuk.co.uk and connect with Nicole at www.instagram.com/a.box.full.of.joy.uk

Chapter Two

To the teen who struggles with their weight

by Emma Rimmer

To the teen who struggles with their weight,

I look back now at the emotions I felt, the mistakes I made, and the way I behaved – all because I felt alone, because I felt like an outcast, because I worried too much about what people thought of me.

I'm going to be totally honest with you right now, because you are me 20 years ago, and at the age of 35, you will still worry about what people think of you, just not as much as you do now. You're in for a rollercoaster of a ride over the next 20 years, girl, but you will come out stronger on the other side! I can promise you that!

I know you think I'm talking out my arse. Why wouldn't you? You're 15, and you are already on a rollercoaster. You've been riding it for three years. It started with the news that we were moving away, miles away from the friends and family we grew up with, to a place we had never heard of and struggled to pronounce correctly.

In the months we were mentally preparing for that move to the middle of nowhere, the 'quiet little town,' we lost two members of our family – our great nan and then, a month later, our nan. That was a massive blow to our family. The following seven months involved travelling up and down the country to find a new house, a new school, turning 13, and saying goodbye.

By the time we turn 14, we have started a new school, and language definitely seems to be a barrier. I mean, we didn't move to a new country or anything, but the accent is a challenge! Especially when you don't really know whether your German teacher is speaking German or English!?! It's safe to say that it is not a GCSE we pass, but don't worry; you haven't needed to use German before the age of 35, and I can't see you needing it anytime soon.

You have made some friends in your form, and other kids around school are noticing the "new girl with the London accent," but so have the bullies. There are a few kids out there with stereotypical views, and believe that you are posh and rich because you are from London. They don't know you yet; they don't know where you have come from. The words might hurt, and the physical bullying isn't a joy either, but they don't know that your dad taught you to be tough, to look after yourself. They don't know that you won't be a pushover and that you will stand up to them, even if they are boys; they will learn who you are, and you will gain respect! But you have a rough ride on the way there.

So at 15, with everything going on – puberty, the changes to your body that are being unwelcomingly noticed, the hormones, the emotions you are already experiencing through loss and pain, being bullied, and feeling like you don't belong – you are comfort eating.

Your weight is going to become an issue. It has been up and down like a yo-yo, but so have your emotions and hormones. Your self-esteem and confidence have taken a beating. And again, I must be brutally honest. Weight is still a problem now, but you are dealing with it much better as an adult. You have learned from your mistakes. The mistakes you are about to make …

You speak to Mum. She is your best friend. You have shown her some stretch marks on your stomach, so she will take you to see a doctor to see if you could get something to help with the appearance of the stretch marks. But your appointment does not go well. The doctor tells you that you have stretch marks because you are fat! Mum goes ballistic. She will try to reassure you that you are not fat, but it doesn't stop what happens next.

I told myself it must be true; it came from the doctor, a professional. He knows what he is talking about, right?

Everywhere I looked, I was comparing myself to others, thinking they were comparing themselves to me, having unhealthy conversations with "friends" about weight. These so-called friends would put themselves down to me, calling themselves "fat" when they knew full well they weren't big compared to me, and this made me feel more disgusted with myself.

You'll know whom I mean. You can tell who is using you to make themselves feel better about themselves.

I started to not want to eat; the thought of eating made me feel ill. It was the food's fault I was fat. I thought that if I didn't eat, I would lose weight – simple. I wanted to be skinny like everyone else because in my head, I was the only overweight person I knew. I started by throwing my lunches in the bin. I took a packed lunch to school so I just told Mum I had eaten it. Then, I started skipping breakfast. The only meal I couldn't avoid was dinner, as we sat down to eat as a family. It wasn't long before I made myself sick after meals. I was disgusted with myself. Every time I felt food in my mouth, I hated myself and thought that if the doctor could see I was fat, then so could everyone else.

It will be friends at school who first notice you aren't eating. As a teenager at school, this is whom you spend your time with. They will pick up on things like you not hanging out in the drama department, where everyone who has a packed lunch goes. You don't realise it just yet, but you are lucky to have a handful of good, genuine friends who like you for you, who you won't feel the need to change for. They have your back.

These friends helped me realise that starving myself wasn't doing me any favours. Yes, I lost weight, but when I got the confidence to eat again, I put even more weight on, and then I would want to stop eating again to lose it. After yo-yoing for months, that's when I noticed more stretch marks. I was getting stretch marks from gaining and losing weight quickly. I had to break the cycle.

It will not be easy. That demon in your head is telling you you're fat, you're ugly. Please don't listen. That's easier said than done when it's what you hear every time you look in a mirror or see a reflection of yourself, but is torturing yourself worth it? Who gains in the long run? Not you! Starving yourself is not a healthy way to lose weight.

I know you worry about what people think of you, but listen to your friends checking in on you every day, asking how you're feeling, asking what you've eaten today. Don't get annoyed with them; they aren't trying to mother you – they care! Yes, people outside of your family care about you! And if you are too ashamed to speak to your parents, it's great that you have some close friends to talk to. They ask if you fancy what's in your lunch box today or if you want to go to the cafeteria instead to see what's on. You have your pocket money; it's okay, you will make choices for yourself. You will realise you are the boss! You are in control. Don't let that demon beat you!

Your friends encourage you to walk home from school with them. You want to spend more time with them. They make you feel good. They make you feel happy. You also start getting off the bus a few stops earlier in the morning to meet up with them.

This feeling of being accepted, having friends again, not being judged on what you look like or where you come from will give you a boost in confidence, and little do you know, but this extra walking is making you lose weight and tone up! You will feel good about yourself again, I promise.

I'll let you in on a secret, too. You will fall in love with exercise in the next 10 years – even running! I know, you're laughing at me now. Yes, the girl who dodges cross-country will love to run! How ironic!

Don't be too hard on yourself. What the doctor didn't tell you was that stretch marks can develop through puberty because of

Chapter Three

To the teen who does not know her worth

By Kasey Alice

To the teen who does not know her worth,

Content warning: sexual abuse

I know you did not expect things to work out this way. It all started so innocently. There is no way you could have predicted what happened.

I know you felt invisible at school. Seeing other people who had big friendship groups and others who had close friends was painful. Striving for friendship and somehow still fading into the background unnoticed was hard. It felt like a lot of kids at school only knew your name and nothing else about you, nor did they care to get to know you.

Being invisible at school made even the simple things hard. Breakfast and lunch, when everyone sat at a table with their friends, you sat alone. Anxiety crept up every time you walked out of the lunch line with a tray full of food, scanning the cafeteria for a place where you could belong long enough to eat your food.

Far above those dreaded times were class breaks when you wished you could just stay at your desk. It would have been different if you had friends. As you scanned for a place to belong amongst chatting peers, where you would not be in the way or noticed, the lies you believed rang with clarity. "I have no friends. No one sees me. I don't matter. I'm not worth talking to."

And then, something unusual happened. There was a boy who liked you! You were fine with not being seen by boys and a little shocked that someone liked YOU.

When he asked you out, you were excited and nervous and didn't even want to go to school because it would be so awkward to see him now. The title "girlfriend" made you feel weird. How was a girlfriend supposed to act? Let's be honest; you made it really awkward and didn't speak to him, or even look his way, the first day you were dating. For the next week, you blushed anytime he looked at you or came to talk to you.

You told yourself it was because you were awkward. But was that the truth, or was it because the relationship wasn't right? Either way, you didn't know what would happen. It all started slowly, almost unnoticeably. That is the way most of these relationships start. It's a slow degradation.

A few months in, he was driving you home from school daily, and just before he got to your driveway, he told you to look up out of the sunroof. As you leaned over and looked at what he was pointing at, he kissed you on the cheek. You were not expecting that. He knew you were not ready. That is why he had to distract you and then steal a kiss. Your face flushed redder than a tomato, and you instantly clung to the door and looked out the window, saying nothing for the rest of the car ride home.

He laughed at your reaction, thinking nothing of it. You didn't even glance his way when he parked the car; you opened the door and left without a word. It should have been a red flag that he would intentionally steal a kiss instead of asking for one and waiting until you were ready. It's not your fault that you didn't see the warning signs. They can be tricky to see when you are involved in the relationship.

I wish I could say that was the only red flag that you missed, but it wasn't; there were many. Remember when he was so crabby about you getting a job because you would not have enough time with him? That was a red flag, too. When he wanted to control all of your time and expected you to sacrifice your needs and desires to appease him, that was manipulation. That is why when you joined wrestling cheerleading, he screamed, "You already work! We will not have any time together!"

Another form of manipulation was when he yelled at you for looking at a wrestler. He said he was watching your eyes and saw you "check him out." You had to defend yourself against what he "knew" you were thinking.

You don't need to defend yourself over what people think you are thinking.

When in a bad relationship, it starts slowly, and then once you think the first level of misbehavior is "normal," usually there is another level added to it. It's a slow breakdown of your boundaries, a slow breakdown of who you are and what you stand for. As the relationship advances, it is easy to become consumed by the relationship, as the other things you were interested in have faded away, but the truth is that they have been slowly pushed away.

Remember when he would bounce the basketball off your head multiple times? You tried to be a good sport about it... and then he would do it again, and again, and again. When you were trying to block, he would run up to do a layup, bounce the ball off your forehead, catch it, and make a basket... then persisted to brag about it. That was the misbehavior going to the next level, where you accepted something you would have never accepted right away in the relationship. It's hard to notice when you are slowly being broken down.

You were ready to step out of the relationship multiple times but knew that he could make high school a living hell for you... so you stayed. You tried to stand strong for so long. For over a year, you stood strong, but the pressure never stopped. You couldn't get away from the pressure. Truth be told, you were not sure how to get away from him.

You reached out to your sister, cousin, and a close friend that he was pressuring you to have sex with him. They believed you and even reached out for you. They told his mum. She then stopped you in the entrance way as you both were leaving the house to go to a sports game. As soon as he walked out the door, she asked the question, "Is he pressuring you to have sex with him?"

You felt trapped in the entranceway. He was going to walk in the door anytime, and you did NOT feel comfortable having that conversation with her! She was not a safe person to talk about that with. What would she do? Talk to him, and then he would be angry with you, livid, and probably start doing crazy stuff.

You were doing the right thing and reaching out for help. Instead of staying in a relationship where you need help, next time, leave the relationship, get space, and figure it out before entering back into the relationship (if that is what you choose). It's best to stop things before it goes further... you didn't know that it was going to go further. If I could step back in time, I would scoop you up and move you through life, so you didn't have to experience what came next.

Then, it happened.

You knew it shouldn't have happened, but the constant pressure finally made you collapse. You tried to think of all the reasons not to, but the reasons were not good enough. Even his mom's rule of having the door open did not stop him. You felt like running away. Physically, you couldn't run, but you did mentally, staring at the wall, almost to pretend that it was not happening. You didn't know it, but that is called disassociation. It's how you were protecting yourself and putting distance between you and a hurt that was too big to comprehend.

He asked you, "Did you like that?" after he finished, and you pressed your lips together and held back most of the tears with no words to respond. Although you tried to hold them back, a few drifted down your cheek. He didn't notice. You felt horrible because you wanted to wait until marriage. It felt like a piece of you was taken, and it was. It was a hurt you hid deep down, not sharing it with anyone as you questioned who you really were and what you stood for.

Please remember that you are not defined by your past. It does not change who you are. With time, you will learn to stand strong. This lesson, as hard as it was, will create a deep resolve (fire) inside of you to not let the influences of others sway your obedience to your inner truth.

Your inner fire started burning a little brighter after that day. Slowly, the feelings you had for him turned into hate, but you felt you still couldn't get away. You tried to break up multiple times, and he kept showing up, calling, and pressuring you back into dating him. Your parents hired him to do some fencing and wood splitting at your home, so he was at school when you got to school and at your house when you came home. He also drove the extra 20 minutes to sit in the lobby of your work, just to make sure you were not talking with any other guys.

One day, when there was another man in the lobby, he sat there with his arms crossed for almost your entire shift until the other man left. Instead of letting his actions wear you down, you channelled them into your inner fire. With every overbearing action, your fire grew. You didn't know what was happening at the time, but you were slowly building your inner strength to endure what happened next.

Then, you decided no more. If he would not let you break up with him, then you would switch the game and make him WANT to break up with you. You knew it wouldn't happen without a fight, but for one of the first times, you realized you were worth fighting for.

He turned everyone against you – your sister, your cousin, the people at your school, all the people that you spent time with. Your sister and cousin were yelling at you because you didn't want to be with him. They said that it is your fault and that they couldn't believe that you would be so mean and selfish. You felt like there was no safe place to go and no one on your side. It worked; you broke up, but it didn't stop him.

Then, a mutual friend showed up at work. You didn't know his intentions; you were happy to see him. As you chatted, he asked about your plans for the night after work. He started asking you whom you were hanging out with and what plans you had for the rest of the week. You were mid-sentence when you realized he wasn't asking to be friendly. He was gathering information for your ex.

The fear and realization of what was going on stole your voice as you looked him dead in the eyes for a few seconds of silence and then walked into the back of the shop. Only workers were allowed there, so you took a few deep breaths. Yet, feelings of being trapped weighed on you, so you walked out the back door of the shop, knowing full well that your mutual friend was probably still in the lobby.

Instantly, you knew it was a bad idea as you saw your ex's car parked a few feet from the back door. You instinctively put your foot in the back door, so it would not close and lock you out. He was leaning on the passenger door with his arms crossed over his chest, eyes locked on you. There was no way you could walk out of the door without being in close contact with him. You went back inside and shut the door as fast as you had opened it. The tears couldn't be held back anymore. Your ex was parked at the back exit, and his friend was in the lobby. You felt trapped. You didn't understand why he was making your life a living hell, but in time, you learned that manipulation comes in many forms, and when you stand against it, it usually gives one last fight before it is broken.

A few hours later, you walked to your car after the shift, double and triple checking the parking lot. Luckily, they were gone.

The next two months were a freedom you enjoyed to the fullest. He was no longer showing up at your house or stalking you at work. As the summer ended and college was starting, you thought it would be the fresh start to life that you needed, only to find out that your ex's dorm was THREE DOORS AWAY from yours. But worse yet, he still had it out for you. As he had been meeting people in the dorm, he was telling them you were his ex-girlfriend and that the reason you broke up was because he found you in bed with another man.

So as you insecurely entered the next chapter of your life, you entered with a title of "hoe" with the surrounding people already judging you. Questions hit you as you asked yourself, "Is it possible to change locations and still have nothing change? Is my new chapter going to be a repeat of the last few years of drama and not being able to get away from this man?"

Then, the text came, "Give me back that bullet." He had given you a bullet earlier that year and said that it was because of you that he was still around. He was going to kill himself, but because of you, he didn't. He was asking for the bullet; he wanted to commit suicide because he saw you talking to a different guy. Your answer was "no," but that did not stop him from pushing the limits once again. He said, "Well, if you won't give me back the bullet, then I will find another way to do it. My car goes over 100 miles an hour. I can use that."

You spent the night texting him, trying to talk some sense into him and make sure that he did not make the fatal mistake of suicide. You didn't recognize then that this was another attempt at manipulating you, making you feel responsible for his actions, forcing you to give him your time and attention with the threat of his life held over you.

As you handled the situation, the pressure and all his mounting demands piled until you broke. You walked out of the dorm, through the snow-covered parking lot, and into your car. You called your parents, and after a few minutes of crying to them, getting no words out, explained that he was going to commit suicide if you didn't do what he wanted (date him). They called his parents and let them know he was threatening suicide... and finally, as you hung up the phone, something broke deep inside of you.

You didn't know what broke at the time, but instantly, you felt a shift. What broke was his power over you. Your inner resolve to stand strong grew into a raging fire, and in a moment, you decided:

Never again to stay quiet and play down your skills so he could gloat and brag.

Never again would you sacrifice the things you wanted to fit his schedule better.

Never again would you let him pressure you into something that you didn't want.

Never again would you let the words he spoke about you form how you acted. Never again would you care about what he threatened to do and how he wanted to control you.

Control only works if you let it.

Don't worry about rumours that are spread about you. Show up authentically as yourself, and eventually, your character will speak louder than his lies.

He can threaten to commit suicide. In the end, that is his choice. It will never be your choice. Do not act like you have ownership over that choice. If he used it as a control mechanism in the past, he will use it as a control mechanism in the future. Refuse to live in fear and allow someone else to manipulate you by saying you cause their choices. That is a lie. You did well when you told his parents. They can handle the situation.

You have the freedom to live by your morals and convictions. Do not let other people pressure you into doing things you are not okay with. Your body is not a playground for other people. Wait for someone who honours and cherishes you.

Choose to forgive yourself.

God's grace covers you. He forgave you for the things that happened. Now, choose to forgive yourself for letting the relationship continue for so long. Give yourself grace for past mistakes and believe in your future potential. Do not let this bad experience colour your life or how you look at the world.

Every experience in life is something to learn from, so take the lessons you have learned and continue on your journey. Your path is bright, and your future promising. You've got this.

Love Kasey

About Author

KASEY ALICE

Kasey Alice is a woman who is remembering how to dream. She is healing her past and standing for her future. She is a gentle warrior who stands for the broken and speaks encouragement over others. She has a fire within her that will not go out. The fire burns to stand for what is right and to show her brokenness to the world so that others know it's okay to be broken. Her words to you are, "You can still thrive in this life even if you have situations that have broken you in the past. You were born to flourish; keep going."

Chapter Four

To the teen who is hiding behind a mask

by Charlotte Lewington

To the teen who is hiding behind a mask ...

Has anyone ever told you how brave, loved, and wanted you are? Has anyone really listened to you, asked how you are feeling, and validated those thoughts? Have they told you recently that you were born with amazing talents and gifts that will positively impact the world?

I know what you are capable of, and I want to tell you... you can do anything that you put your mind to, if only you believe in yourself, your skills, and your capabilities. I know this because the future is full of possibilities if you learn how to take off the mask you are hiding behind, and step into the authentic version of you. I want you to know you are loved and are good enough, never let anyone tell you differently.

To the teen who is hiding behind the mask to fit in, I write this letter because I remember the times that triggered you to hide away, to lose your voice and not feel you were a part of anything. I remember the times that would make you think that the world would be a better place with you not being there.

From the minute they knew you were coming into the world, you were defying all the odds and setting a bigger mission for yourself. I mean, few people can say that their mum was sterilised and still fell pregnant, but you were that child. You proved to many that you were a fighter before you arrived into the world.

From a young age, life tested your resilience. It was here that life changed. As soon as you found out your brother was terminally ill with a brain tumour, you knew that life would never be the same. An assortment of emotions ran through your head. Finding out news like that at such a young age was mind blowing; how could you possibly comprehend the meaning of what was going on?

People tell you that as a child, you don't understand; you see things from a child's perspective. What they don't know is that as children, we may not understand what is going on, but we know that something is going on. In that moment, being a little child who doesn't understand can be the worst feeling in the world.

I was only three years old when my brother received his diagnosis; of course, that moment is going to change your life. How could that happen to our family? Why is life so cruel? That moment changed the little girl inside of you; it made you grow up very quickly. It was that moment that taught you to understand the unconditional love a parent has for their child. As hard as it was hearing those words, you were able to go on to learn the lesson that would help you turn into the woman you were meant to be – the woman who understood empathy, the pain of loss and loneliness and still rose to overcome everything that was thrown your way.

I still remember that morning when Mum came into the bedroom and told us he was gone – our brother had died peacefully in his sleep at 3:00 in the morning. I still have a vague recollection of going into the school playground one day and telling my friends that it had happened – my brother had died. Too young to understand but wise enough to realise that something was going on.

It was this pivotal moment in life that dented the confidence of the young girl who was growing up. At a crucial time when children are forming relationships and attachments to those around them, you lost one of the closest relationships to you. A brother is there to protect you, to have silly fights with, to play fun games with, to be the uncle to your children, to see you get married, and to share all of life's magical moments with. His death took away all of those things from you at such a young age. Loss is difficult to deal with at any age, but you experienced it when you were only six years old, so don't be too hard on yourself. It is no wonder you learnt to live life hiding behind a mask.

From one traumatic event to the next, the challenging times didn't end there. In secondary school, you had the chance to make new friends, move to a different area, and make a new start for yourself, but it is not the easy task or the fairy-tale ending that some people are lucky to have during their school years.

It is here that people accuse you of lying about losing your brother and make your life very difficult with constant arguments and rumours being spread about you that were not true. There was something new to deal with every day. It is these years that cause you to question yourself as a person and ask, "Why me? Why do all the bad things happen to me?"

Never being picked for the school sports team, not part of the popular group, never believing you were pretty enough or good enough, the constant pressure to look and be a certain way always resonated with me because I never felt like I fit in. I was never the popular girl, and I didn't have many true friends. It is during these times that the comparisons became much more present.

It was seeing the constant posts on Facebook that made me wish I was a part of "that group" – you know, the one that everyone seems to want to be part of.

During my secondary school years, I would constantly try to change myself to fit in with other girls in the class. I changed my accent because I was told I sounded too posh, hid what school I went to before and what my predicted grades were because I didn't want to come across as being too bright. Looking back now, I wish I had the confidence and the voice to be who I was always meant to be, but it took years to realise.

I had tears rolling down my face each night, wondering what was wrong with me. How can one person be so unlikeable? It was so easy to give my power away to others and let them have control over how they made me feel. We live in a world surrounded by ideals. All you have to do is look online and at different media sources, which present us with better versions of just about everything, creating the pressure to strive for more. Is it any wonder so many of us feel like we are not enough?

Growing up today, the fear of missing out is something that I'm sure every young teenager is going to experience in their life. "You totally missed out" were words we heard repeatedly upon arriving at school after another weekend of being alone, not invited to a sleepover that 'everyone who was anyone' was invited to – everyone but you.

So many times, that was the new norm – turning up at school only to hear other people talking about the latest party they had been invited to, the trips to the cinema or bowling. There was always something going on which I was not a part of. I don't know why it bothered me so much. I would tell other people I didn't want to go anyway when, in reality, it bothered me so much and I felt so low about myself that anxiety crept in.

If there is one thing that I want to make you aware of, it's that social media makes you think, "Maybe I should be somewhere else doing something else with someone else." If you always think your happiness is somewhere else, it will never be where you are. Sometimes, the universe has other plans for you, and what you think you're missing out on can actually be a blessing in disguise.

I could probably count on my hands the few times where I felt like I fit in and had made friends, but it would always result in near misses. Remember that time when you were nearly set on fire by those who thought it would be funny? Then, the time they threatened you and took your phone or the time you nearly got beaten up?

There were so many times that you would get let down by people who you thought were friends. Looking back now, it almost feels as though there was a guardian angel looking out for you that turned these events into near misses you escaped from.

During the college years, finally things were starting to look up. You had found an encouraging group of girls that you get on well with, and could finally enjoy going out with people you can trust, and had so many treasured moments and fun times together. There were also so many up and down moments, but you thought, "She is my friend; these things happen. You fight, you make up, that's the joys of being friends with people. You understand each other and accept one another – imperfections and all."

I will never forget the day that I received the news that my friend had been killed in a car crash. In that moment, I was devastated, I couldn't breathe. I was standing in the high street with people looking at me wondering why I had just broken down. Little did they know what was being said on the other end of the phone.

My heart was torn into pieces; there were so many things I wanted to say to her, so many more experiences and memories we were meant to make together, so many questions spinning around in my head – "What had happened? Why did she decide to get in that car? She was so close to her home; why didn't she make it?"

I just kept thinking of the last time I saw her; she had decided she didn't want to do the childcare course anymore and that she was going to do an IT course instead. She was finally happy; she had met someone and knew what she wanted to do with her life.

Why did someone close to me have to die again? Why her? Why is life so unfair?

People are going to come into your life for a reason, a season, or a lifetime. There are many people that you will encounter, and each of them can teach you a valuable lesson, if you look for the lesson being taught. The heartache you go through can strengthen you or destroy you. You have a choice. You can either sit down and cry about things, or you get up and look for the lesson being shown to you.

Crying is our emotional connection with the world. This simple act is often seen as a weakness when it is actually the strength in us. It is okay to cry about things as it is a natural reaction of our body and one that promotes a healthier mind. There is a great quote that says, "Don't forget that you are human. It is okay to have a meltdown, just don't unpack and live there. Cry it out and then refocus on where you are headed." It is important to cry about hard things, but it is important to use them to drive you and not paralyse you.

Sometimes, those lessons are not always clear, and you will feel like giving up, but I am writing about those experiences, so you know you will find the strength to pick yourself up and keep going.

It is in the darkest moments that you must focus on seeing the light. Anyone can be happy, positive, and grateful when everything is going well. But when nothing is going well, that is when we truly need to focus our minds and dig deep.

These experiences that I am talking about have helped me believe that who you surround yourself with will enable you to flourish, especially when you are faced with difficult times. As you grow older, it doesn't matter that your close circle of friends is small. I know these people will always have my back, no matter what, and I want that for you, too. There is no point surrounding yourself with people who don't bring out the best in you and make you want to keep hiding behind the mask.

The people who understand you and accept you for who you are – those are the type of friends that you should surround yourself with. They will be the ones who get you through the tough times and be there to celebrate the good times with you. When you learn to accept your complete self (even the bits that you try to hide), you attract people who accept them, too. You find people who don't make you feel you need to change who you are. I want you to realise that the people that don't understand you are not your sort of people. Not everyone is going to like you, and you need to accept that that is okay.

Follow your heart and live your life as you want to. Look inside of yourself and become self-aware. Find out who you are, who you want to be, what you like. When you look in the mirror, who is the person you see staring back at you? Don't let yourself be defined by the words of other people. Go deep inside yourself and find out what it really means to love yourself from the inside out.

Finally, and most importantly, set boundaries for yourself. People will only treat you according to the standards that you set for yourself. Over the years, I learned to believe in myself and stop settling for second best. That is when life changed for the better. Don't be afraid to say "no" to people and say "yes" to those opportunities that light you up.

You are enough, just as you are. Take off that mask you are hiding behind and embrace every part of you, imperfections and all. You are good enough, you are loved, and life is too short to worry about what other people think. Go out there and create your own future just the way you want to, remembering to always have hope.

Love Charlotte

"We have always held to the hope, the belief, the conviction that there is a better life, a better world, beyond the horizon." – Franklin D. Roosevelt

About Author

CHARLOTTE LEWINGTON

Charlotte Lewington is a well-being coach and executive trainer. Her two passions in life are supporting people and making a positive impact in the world.

From a young age, she always had a love for children and decided to pursue a career within the childcare profession. She became an expert by developing her knowledge with a masters in children and young people. She began to understand how powerful the mind is as well as how your childhood experiences and the impact of social media can affect your confidence and self-esteem as an adult.

Charlotte has gone on further spreading her message by making it her mission to educate people on the importance of mental health and well-being within the early years and beyond. She has gained her experience working with schools, nurseries, and organisations through developing and delivering courses on the subject.

Connect with Charlotte at www.instagram.com/mente_hermosa_academy and visit her website here www.mente-hermosa-academy.com

CHAPTER FIVE

To the teen who is unsure on their path

BY HOLLY FOSTER

TO THE TEEN WHO is unsure on their path in education,

What if I told you that the feeling you have right now, where you're unsure of what you want to do and where you want your career to lead, is NOT a problem? It feels like a lot of pressure to figure out who you want to be and how you want to get there; I get that and let me tell you why in this letter!

I mean, who even knows exactly what they want to study and then do for life and their future career at just seventeen? What if you want to pick something different from A-levels, something you haven't tried before, like psychology? Well, for one, you need to learn how to spell it, and we both know that's not your strong suit.

In school, teachers tell us you go to sixth form after GCSEs. After that, you spend a minimum of three years at university, then you get a job. We don't get taught many alternatives, but this expected education process doesn't work for everyone. Why follow the "norm" and what's "expected" when you can follow your heart, which is screaming at you to stay true to who you are?

Often, throughout life, your head and heart will not be on the same page. Your head thinks more logically, whereas your heart feels with emotions. Over the last seven years, I have learned what it's like to follow my heart and my head, but things turned out better when they aligned with one another. When my heart wasn't in it, my head struggled to understand what I was reaching towards. You didn't follow the "norm." You've completed your GCSEs; I know you're not entirely happy with them, but you passed, and that's an achievement. French is difficult, but you did it! You should be proud of that!

Now, I know how you're feeling, remember; I am you in just seven years, but I've faced HUGE learning curves, and I'm about to tell you that every choice you make is worth it, even the ones that seem tough.

So pick the A-levels you want. I know, you're not ready to leave that school yet; it's where your friends are. So stay. I tell you, a year down the line, you'll be somewhere else. You will not find sixth form easy, believe me. But you are going to LOVE college; it's worth the wait as you needed sixth form to teach you the new goals you wanted to reach, and allow you to appreciate the experience even more.

The jump from GCSE to sixth form was too overwhelming for me, so I went to college to study graphic design. We both know we've always been creative, so this seemed like the perfect opportunity to give it a go. And that's precisely what it was — giving it a go! I didn't know in advance how much I was going to love it, nor did I know I would eventually have my graphic design business called HF Designs a few years later!

At A-Levels, I took the subjects I loved and wanted to learn more and picked up psychology (don't ask anyone to test us on the spelling, though). You have always loved maths, still do, and so with your 'A' in GCSE, this seemed like the right choice. You also love philosophy and ethics and learning why people think how they do with morals, values, and how the world came to be so that was your third. Last but not least, you have a passion for creative writing, therefore, English literature became your fourth choice. All sounds pretty great, huh? And it was, but the dynamics of learning, studying, and movement of friendships changed my entire experience. I didn't dislike the subjects at all, but I couldn't work out how to learn everything, remember to be tested on that subject, and study in a way that worked for me.

By the Christmas of 2015, I dropped psychology, not because I couldn't spell it but because I couldn't retain any of the facts and information. I was interested, sure, but I didn't want to be tested on the matter. I was getting 2/20 in simple class tests on topics we had learned the week before. It's fair to say psychology was not in my future!

I applied for graphic design at college, and by February 2016, they gave me an automatic place to start the following September for the new school year. Now, I could have given up sixth form entirely and just waited until September. But I didn't. I wanted to prove to myself that although I had a "get out of jail free card," I was still going to try my very best at the subjects I was still studying, so I stayed in school. We are not one to just give up because it's hard. You like maths still, and this was problem-solving – just one big problem you had to reach the end of. Even though it was actually Mum's idea to leave school early, as she could see the shift in my happiness and attitude, my determination and ambition had taken over my heart, and I powered through the last few months.

I finished my AS levels with just two grades in the end. I had English and philosophy and ethics, not maths – which crushed me. I had three individual tutors for maths, and I still failed. This became a huge turning point for me, as I thought I just wasn't "academic" enough. Being 'academic' had always seemed like it was a huge deal, that you were not a good enough student if you were not academic. I was frustrated that somewhere in my head I had actually told myself that I wasn't good enough for school. So, after finishing my AS Levels I left sixth form and moved myself away from a place that had caused me so many negative thoughts and emotions, which started to change who I was. I wanted to find me again!

Graphic design sounded like a massive weight off my shoulders by the time September came around. There was no "studying." Research, yes, but no "test" at the end of the course. My time at college was the best three years of my education! I worked so hard that I finished with mostly distinctions and a handful of merits. I completed the first year of my BTEC and moved right onto graphic design HNC, with an HND award that followed because of my efforts and achievements. I was so proud of myself for the grades I had achieved; it was very unlike the disappointment I felt after receiving my GCSE and AS level results. I finally felt like I was really good at something and that I could do graphic design as a career.

After my awful experience in sixth form, it put me off wanting to go to university, and my parents certainly didn't want to force it on me after how much I had changed in the past. However, thanks to my HNC and HND, I only needed to attend university for one year, a top-up year, to get my whole degree in graphic design. And that sounded pretty perfect to me! So that's what I did.

I joined university at the third-year level to top up the rest of my degree and completed the year successfully. Now, like sixth form, I didn't enjoy uni like I thought I would. But I was determined to get a degree, so I worked as hard as I could to get one! I was the first person in my whole family who'd ever earned a degree; that feels pretty special, and I am so proud of myself!

I graduated three years ago, and since then, I have worked in a few different jobs, including social media, creative assistant, and a kids shoe fitter (we're still doing this job; it's a lot of fun!). My proudest achievement is that I run my own successful business, HF Designs. I'm a creative designer specialising in branding for a multitude of companies. I also support parenting businesses that care for the well-being, mental health, and education of young people. My mission is to spread happiness to loads of people in as many ways as I can through my creative design services.

HF Designs is now one year old, and I am so proud to have gone into business for myself and met incredible ladies and businesses who support me and whom I have worked with. The community is a loving business family, and I have grown drastically as a person and in business because of it.

When I was seventeen, I decided I never wanted to go to university, and I never wanted to work for myself, but I have done both things. I am so pleased that I did! You'd be surprised how the things you didn't want to do become some of the best decisions you were brave enough to face and will shape who you become.

So that's our story. You and I are both Holly Foster, and we don't follow the "norm" or what they expected of us as a teenager in school. My higher education story was not straightforward, and I needed to work very hard to keep powering through and get results I was proud of. Our journey moulds us into the person we become. I have learned to follow my heart and do what makes me happy. I am still discovering who I want to be, and we are always learning more about ourselves each day; for example, I run now, and I used to despise the thought of running! I know that if we follow our values, happiness and being our true self will follow.

Love Holly

P.S. If you're reading this and feel you can relate – maybe you're struggling to reach the expectations you have set for yourself and don't know what to do – remember, there is always another way to get where you want to be. My mum always tells me, "There's always a solution." It used to annoy me when I was younger, but I've grown to love it, as now, I understand it, and finding a new way to do something can open even more opportunities to lead you to your happiest self.

About Author

Holly Foster

Holly is a creative designer with a passion to help people who help people! With a degree in graphic design, six years experience in the graphics industry, and 10 years of experience working with parents and children, she finds herself acting as the "Big Sister" of businesses, bridging the gaps between parenting businesses and their ideal clients – children.

Holly has been fortunate to have lived a happy, upbeat life and feels that everyone deserves to be happy for at least 90% of their life. And that is what she aims to do when working with her customers – spread joy to not just themselves, but to their own customers, too. It's her biggest goal! Holly helps businesses boost the connection with their customers, allowing them to help them on a deeper, more meaningful level through the art of graphic communication and design.

If you have a business that's bursting to boost the happiness, confidence, and well-being of those you work with and those around you, then please connect with her at https://www.facebook.com/hollyfosterdesigns or https://www.instagram.com/holly_foster_designs/ because she wants to work with YOU!!

Chapter Six

To the teen who has lost their sense of self

By Eva Olave Martinez

To The Teen who lost their sense of self while being pulled in all directions.

I remember the day it all began. I remember standing in the playground, confused, frozen, with loud voices deafening my ears to the point of despair. Children shouted, "You don't have a mum, you don't have a mum." That hurt. I was only six... I did not believe them.

It was only when I went outside that the realisation hit... why didn't my mum come and pick me up? My uncle was there to explain that my mum would no longer look after my sister and I, and we were going to live with my grandmother. They didn't tell me how or why she had died; they just said, "she is gone," like a whisper in the wind, leaving me completely broken.

Did it actually happen that way? Or was this a dream (more like a nightmare) that my mind kept as a reminder of the worst day possible?

I am not even sure.

I felt empty, as if I had lost all sense of myself; the core of my foundations in life was shaken. The years passed, and despite trying, I struggle to find many memories. It's as if I only existed, numb to the world. Suddenly, happiness was gone; the laughter had quieted, and I no longer had the smile of my mother to keep me warm.

There is, however, a powerful memory of me and my sister etched into my memory about six months after my mum's passing, when we were taken from my grandmother to my dad and my paternal grandmother. My paternal grandmother had very strong views regarding dummies, and when it was time to go to bed, my paternal grandmother refused to give my 2-year-old sister her dummy. My sister and I shared a double bed. When she could not sleep and was continually crying out for her dummy, my dad got up and really reprimanded her, ordering her to sleep. That is the only time my dad lost his temper with us, and I really feel that it weighs heavily on his heart as well.

My sister's cry broke my heart, and all I could do was cuddle her until she fell asleep, which seemed like an eternity. My senses kept the memory of that moment, and I remember the colours, sounds, and smells as if it was yesterday. I remember a brown and red checked blanket over the bed and how it felt when placing my hand on it.

This memory became clear to me when I was your age, a teen, just as the real conflicts of my existence surfaced, coinciding perhaps with my father's remarrying (or maybe it's just that when you are a fully grown adult, teen years are often as far back as you can remember). My sister and I had to, once again, leave what we called home and separate from our second mum, our maternal grandmother. It had taken a while to feel safe at my grandmother's house and now we had to move again. I remember asking my grandmother to leave the passage light on so I could relax enough to sleep and that had been the routine from then on.

Some days my grandfather would tell us stories of when he was growing up and his calm voice and funny stories would stay with us in our dreams. I will not tell my grandchildren how he used to climb the neighbour's tree to steal some figs, in case it gives them any ideas.

However, your mum is not there to have your back, decisions do not revolve around you anymore. You just tag along, pulled in all directions. So at the age of 12, my sister and I went to live with my dad and stepmother and had to get used to new ways of doing things. There was no longer the safety of leaving the light on in the hallway and even the door was closed behind us by my stepmother, as if that would get rid of us somehow.

What you had to say was not always welcome and certainly not the hundred million questions that your brain needed to satisfy. In order to feel safe back then you needed to know what was going to happen next. This didn't seem like a priority to the adults around you and your constant chatter just resembled noise in the end.

I felt like what I wanted was not a priority and only accommodated if it fit with the schedule the grown-ups had.

I wanted to know the answers. What have I done wrong? Why did she leave me? As if her passing was something my mother could have controlled. Even though the answers couldn't satisfy what my heart really wanted - to have her back with us. I still wanted to be heard.

I have always been sensitive, and the uncertainty and unfinished grief sent my body into overdrive and created allergies to things that had not been a problem before. There really is such a link between our mental and physical health. I suffered some kind of scalp build-up that made me lose bunches of hair. I suffered pneumonia for a month, and my allergies were out of control (not that I knew it was an allergy), and I felt lightheaded almost all the time. Everyone thought I just caught colds easily, but I remember thinking, "I wonder what it would be like to live without the itchiness of a runny nose."

Somehow, everything was heavy on my body and so will be on yours. Even if you hear comments like, "Goodness, you seem like you were born tired" or "You are so slow," try not to take it to heart – people around you will not understand.

You carry a heavy burden that is going to take years to shed, and whatever step you take will be an almighty one. But believe me, you will get there.

You realise that everything you achieved is yours. Despite the setbacks, despite the mistakes, despite the guilt of growing beyond the people who helped you, you are still you. You still deserve to be happy and do the things that make you happy.

You do not owe anyone anything.

It is good to be grateful to anyone who helps you along the way, but that is what we are meant to do as humans. We are meant to help each other and benefit from kindness; the connections and the ripple effects of kindness will carry on forevermore.

For years, I thought that to keep people in my life, I had to be extremely nice and accommodating, even putting them before myself, but that is unsustainable. I used to think that if my mum could leave me, so would everyone else. The fear of abandonment is hard to shake off, but people have proved me wrong. Some friends and family have stood by me through thick and thin. You never know who could become your "heart sister" – not by blood but by love. So it is worth giving people a chance. Be open to connections because other family members do genuinely care, and if you are lucky, you will find friends that will understand as well.

Despite it all, I kept up with my studies relatively well, until I got to sixth form, and then, I had a decision to make. By this point, I had exhausted all help. I saw myself as a burden. A decision needed to be made in order to carry on with my life, but I was overwhelmed with emotions, and my head was a mess.

I thought I wanted to be a chemical engineer because I liked chemistry, and science was my strong subject, but I did not make the grades to get into university. It left me in limbo; my future was hanging in the balance.

The pressure to decide was too strong, and the suggestion of a year abroad before coming back to retake the exams didn't seem such a bad idea.

Therefore, I left Spain to learn English in the UK for a year – a bit of a drastic action, I know.

It was hard, and I cried.

I cried because I missed my family.

I cried because I missed my friends.

I cried because living in a foreign country and learning the language was hard.

I cried because deep down, I knew that without your mum, you are on your own.

It might not be for you, but believe me when I say the people I met gave me a new perspective in life and a new angle from which to look at myself. As they say, we see ourselves through the eyes of others. The interactions I had were incredibly positive and gave me motivation and encouragement to believe in myself.

Even if it is just a change in scenery that is required, every new encounter with different people will help your healing. If you are always striving for perfection, you will always fall short. But the time will come when you realise the goodness, the progress you have made, and that will give you a new-found admiration for yourself and your siblings.

So trust that things will happen for a reason and follow the agenda that life has for you. Losing a parent early on can have devastating effects, but the experiences you had will open your eyes to details that others take for granted or cannot even see.

I know you hold no grudges because that is not you, and that is wonderful.

The adults who looked after me and my sister did what they could under the circumstances, and you will thrive, regardless. Because when one door closes, another one will open, and you will be happy. I know that even more so, as now that I work for a paint manufacturer and work with chemical engineers, I see that with my allergies, it would not have been the right place.

I can only speak for my sister, but connecting and strengthening the bond, listening to each other's pain, cheering on each other's little wins, despite being in different countries, was extremely helpful. Your siblings are the ones who truly understand your pain, even if the pain is felt in different intensities. They know the hole you carry in your heart and what it means to have a missing connection (with your mum).

It was not until my maternal grandmother, our second mum, died that I truly connected with my sister and found peace. She understood what it meant to have lost, for the second time, the most important person in our lives. Our grandma was the strongest person I have ever known. Despite her loss, she did not hesitate to make room in the house for us. We were 6 and 2 years old, and while we felt the loss and changes, she covered us with her love, so we could shelter under her wing for a while. She loved to sing and dance and wouldn't hesitate to twirl us around in the kitchen when a song she liked played on the radio. The Lambada was one of our favourites. I was 17 years old when it came out and those are the things I want to remember; the laughter and magic that she would always bring into my life.

When everyday life was not so appealing, escaping into my imagination was a much better option, drawing, colouring, writing and escaping into nature.

My dad did what he could under the circumstances but definitely taught us to find peace within nature. We climbed mountains, swam in the sea, fished for crabs and shrimps, looked for mushrooms in the forest, and heard a cuckoo for the first time. However, there were many people that had a say in our life, and somehow, we put our feelings on hold.

They say children are resilient, but my view is that they do not have a choice besides bottling it up and carrying on. So try to speak about the grief or anything else you feel as often as you can with people who understand. It is the only way to heal.

Nobody will fill the void of a missing mother's touch, but you will find people, be it friends or family, who will try and will do a great job if you let them.

Very sensitive people like myself and maybe you, need stable connections to feel safe, but it should not come at the price of your own self. The importance of boundaries comes to mind, as people will take advantage. I found this difficult because of my strong desire to find someone to fill the empty space inside me, but I learned the hard way. Nobody is more important than you are. Don't give out more energy than you have for yourself, and do the things you like to do.

Listen to your body for signs of exhaustion and emotional overload. You are fighting your demons, processing your grief, and healing. Be kind to yourself. Getting over the grief is draining, even in years to come, although you will see it gets better with time.

You do not need permission to rest and get your energy back, nor do you have to listen to conversations and topics you find deeply upsetting. Be kind to yourself.

You cannot fight your nature, but you can embrace it and thrive. I entrusted my deepest being to dogs, and they have never let me down. Connect with people who appreciate your sensitivity and who are worthy of your trust. Allow yourself to trust, one step at a time.

For years, I said to myself that I would not have any children because if anything happened to me, I did not want them to suffer. I am glad I did not listen to that negative thought. I did not become a mum until I was 30, but it was well worth it. I loved it, and it helped me to find that mum-daughter bond I was missing, almost making me whole again. I understand it might not be the answer for everyone, so do not rush into it unless you are sure. Weigh the pros and cons for you. It is not a decision to take lightly.

As a coping mechanism, I like to be as informed as possible of what is happening around me, so I can prepare for any eventuality. I know I cannot control everything, but it helps me to keep my worries at bay. Eventually, you will let go of all fear and be free. "Whatever will be will be, and you will be fine" is a motto I share with my children, and I found keepsakes very helpful as a reminder that I had people that cared about me. Do the same if it helps you.

I hope you find this helpful and you can allow love to enter your life because it certainly is all around you.

Love Eva

About Author

EVA OLAVE MARTINEZ

Eva is originally from Spain but travelled to UK to learn English and liked it so much that she stayed to study her BA (Hons) degree in business studies with marketing. She has primarily worked in finance in the manufacturing sector, specialising in credit management, but having her own children opened up a whole new world of interests.

Despite growing up without her mum, she wanted to give all the love to her children that she thought she missed out on. She enrolled in Cache Level 3 Child Development, did a paediatric first aid course, and started her journey in teacher training. She believes her children gave her a second chance at life and helped her grow into the confident, resilient, and warm-hearted person she is today. When her own children grew up, she wanted to help other children and families be as happy as she had been and started "In the Clouds Bookshop" selling Usborne children's books, attending schools and afterschool clubs with reading events, and helping with "Dreams a story at a time." Connect with her on https://www.instagram.com/inthecloudsbookshop and visit https://inthecloudsbookshop.co.uk/

CHAPTER SEVEN

To the teen whose friend died by suicide

BY CASSIE SWIFT

TO THE TEEN WHOSE friend died by suicide ...

Content warning: suicide

The names used in this letter have been changed to preserve anonymity.

I am so sorry for what you are going through. All of the feelings you are currently experiencing are normal. The shock, the guilt, the sadness, the numbness, the wanting to hide away, the not knowing what to say to anyone – ALL of your feelings are normal, and it is okay to feel the way you do. Suicide is not an easy thing to accept or understand.

George was quite a character, you didn't always see eye to eye, but then what teens get on all the time? Especially when, if you so much as look at a boy, you must be going out with him.

George was an only child and was very well spoken. The quirky way he'd say his name very much like James Bond always made you smile. It still does! You remember how talented George was; his piano skills were out of this world. He played in all the school performances, and he played professionally for different things. He was more talented than his music teachers. He also had a radio station and a professional set up at home. All of this made a perfect recipe for bullying and jealousy. George, like yourself, would just shrug it off... or at least that's what you thought he was doing.

It was year 9 just before Christmas. The year was already full of so much extra stress – choosing which subjects you wanted to study at GCSE level, preparing for KS3 SATS, not to mention all the hormone changes, emotional changes, and bodily changes. Things were pretty tough going already. Being a teenager isn't easy, as no one seems to understand, do they?

By the way, I just want to say, don't worry when you pick which GCSE subjects to study. These subjects are not going to be the be-all and end-all for how your life will turn out. Choose things you enjoy doing and go from there. Anyway, I went off on a tangent there – something I'm still excellent at doing. Back to the story of George...

You and George would chat a fair bit; you'd often be put in the same groups for things, so you had a good friendship. But not everyone in your form class, or year group for that matter, were as friendly. The things they would say were just awful.

The saying "sticks and stones may break my bones, but words will never hurt me" is rubbish. There were times you would rather have been hit and had it over and done with, rather than the nasty words that continuously go around in your head. You now know that those who bully others have their own insecurities, and it is a reflection of them and not of you.

I know that doesn't help when you are on the receiving end of bullying. It's not okay to bully people; in these times, you must speak up and tell an adult if this is happening, so that all the pieces can be put together and the right course of action taken.

It was the first Friday in December, about a week before his 14th birthday, when George came into school. You noticed people teasing George, and then you saw what it was all about. George had marks on his neck. People were teasing him about having a girlfriend. The marks didn't look like what they were insinuating because the marks were on each side. When you asked him, he said his shirt was too tight, and it had rubbed. You were just 14 so thought nothing more of it.

It was a busy time, you and George were in the same group working on a project. You were staying after school and going in before school to make sure that you had it right. It was a stressful time. You had to show it on the last Tuesday afternoon before Christmas so wanted to get as much practice in as possible. You were all rehearsing before school that Tuesday. It was all planned and organised.

That Tuesday, you arrived in school at 7.50 a.m. as did the rest of the group, but George didn't show. This was really unusual. You weren't happy about it and moaned to your other friends. The performance was today, and you couldn't do it if George wasn't there! The bell went for the start of school, and as you made your way to the form class, you were really not happy at all. Your form tutor was there and asked you all to sit down in your places. The head of year came in, which was weird, as you had assembly to go to. This was really unsettling, and you sensed something wasn't right.

The head of year started to speak: "I have come to talk to you about an incident involving one of your classmates who isn't here today." Your mind flicked. There were a few people who were off quite a bit, and your eyes scanned the room to see who wasn't in.

"You may have noticed that George isn't in today," she continued. You were so confused at this point; what on earth was she going to say? Had he been in an accident? Was he okay? What had happened? But nothing prepared you for what came next. Writing this so many years later, I am still able to recall that day in so much detail, it is like I go back in time.

"Yesterday, after school, when George's dad got home, he found that George had taken his own life."

The room fell silent. No one moved.

"It was too late to do anything; he had died," she started crying, and like someone had un-paused a movie, the sobbing started around the room. You sat in shock, shaking; the wave of guilt for moaning about George not being at school when he was dead felt all-consuming.

The questions started. "How did it happen?" was the first one. The answer sent chills down your spine. "He hung himself."

The words echoed around your head, tears stinging your cheeks. Nothing seemed real; this could not actually be happening. It was as if you'd soon wake up from this nightmare, and everything would be absolutely fine.

It wasn't fine; this was happening. George had killed himself. He was dead. His birthday was only four days ago. How could a 14-year-old be dead? How did no one notice anything?

The atmosphere in the room was awful. People were either screaming, sobbing, shaking, or sitting in complete silence. The head of year continued, "The rest of year 9 are being told in assembly now, but as his form class, we wanted to tell you separately. You won't be expected to continue with lessons, and if anyone needs any support, please do ask."

That was it! Please do ask, FOR WHAT EXACTLY!? Your friend had killed himself, and you were told to ask if you needed help. It was the most stupid sentence in the history of stupid sentences. Twenty-eight 13/14-year-olds were told that a member of their form had died by suicide, and you were told to ask for help!

The rest of that week was a blur. It was the last week of term before the Christmas holidays, but no one celebrated. George's death hadn't really sunk in.

You spoke to your friends about it, asking why nobody had noticed, why nobody had done something. Then it hit you like a great wave of fire, and in an instant, you blamed yourself.

The week before, when George had come into school with marks around his neck, you hadn't realised and believed his shirt was too tight! You were so stupid; obviously, he had tried before. It was his way of asking for help, but all he got was teased or people like you believing his shirt was too tight! As soon as you realised, you tell the head of year. You had to give a formal statement about this as there would be an inquest to gather evidence from many different places to give an "accurate" cause of death.

If you had told a teacher the week before, George might still be here; why didn't you say anything? The adult me will tell you why you didn't say anything. It was because you were just 14. You were a teenager who asked a question and got what seemed like a feasible answer. As a teenager, you don't question it any further. There was NOTHING you could have done to have changed this, nothing at all. The guilt will eat away at you if you let it, and the truth is if someone wants to end their life, they will. It is certainly not the job of a teenager to spot signs of what may be going on and piece it all together – that is for trained adults to do.

This is a very difficult time for you; the shock and the guilt is affecting you. You aren't able to sleep or even go upstairs by yourself because of the images you see from the loft. Are you feeling anything like this; are you having flashbacks? Is the sight of certain things making you feel sick or anxious? Does even the sound of their name make you burst into uncontrollable tears or violently shake?

If so, firstly, it is okay, and it is a normal reaction; there is nothing "wrong" with you. Secondly, it is now that you need to ask to see the school counsellor and reach out for some support. Grief can be a lonely journey, but there are people who will be able to support and help you once you speak out. It is such an awful time for you, but people did help in the best way they could. Your mum was there giving cuddles and allowing silence – no questioning, just being there. And your friends at school who knew how you felt gave you hugs and wiped away tears when you needed it but also understood that, at times, you needed space, and that was okay, too.

The change in dynamics was astounding; everyone looked out for one another more, and you all came together in your sorrow to remember George and realise that things can build up and affect people more than you have any idea.

I wish I could tell you that this will all go away, but I can't. Losing someone to suicide is a HUGE deal, and as a teenager especially, this trauma will impact the rest of your life BUT not all in a bad way.

You learnt how precious life is. You learnt that it's important to be kind because what you say can be internalised and have a long term impact on people.

As a result of losing someone by suicide, you will be extra careful with words. You will be kind and listen to people when they aren't feeling great. You will be so aware of the changes in people and notice if they have unexplained marks on them, and you will go on to help other teenagers with their struggles.

Your story will be told, and it will help others experiencing similar things. They will know they aren't alone and that things will get easier over time. Your sadness will help others, which itself is an incredible gift. So be kind to yourself, let go of the guilt, and know that you are only a teenager. It is the adults who need to help and support you, and if they don't, ASK!

You are not alone, and you are strong. You will go on to tell your story, and with that, the memory of George will not be lost. Never forget that you are not alone in this; there are specially trained bereavement and trauma counsellors who can help as well as your friends, once you speak up and ask for that support. It is the bravest thing you can do at this time, and it will help you in your journey of grief to be able to navigate it and begin to try and process the events that have happened.

To my teenage self... I want you to let go of the guilt. George wouldn't want you carrying it around with you; that isn't what he wanted.

Love Cassie

About Author

CASSIE SWIFT

Cassie is a passionate children's mental health advocate and a children's and teens' life coach within her business True You Children's Life Coaching. Cassie is also the founder and organiser of the Children's Mental Health Matters Summit - and also a single mummy to three young, beautiful, caring, and mischievous girls.

As a child herself, Cassie experienced bullying throughout her entire school life, and due to this, she obviously didn't enjoy school. Cassie wishes that there had been a children's life coach available for her to have turned to, because as a result, over the years, her mental health deteriorated. This is not something anyone would wish for a child, and no child deserves to feel this way or experience what she went through.

Visit her website www.trueyouchildrenslifecoaching.co.uk and connect with her at https://www.facebook.com/TrueYouChildrensLifeCoaching

CHAPTER EIGHT

To the teen who is in foster care

BY JANE MILLER

TO THE TEEN WHO is in foster care,

Content warning: physical and sexual abuse

I know that feeling!! Your body, stiff with frustration. Your head is so full with voices telling you different things. You don't know what to think and feel like you are going crazy. That butterfly-sick feeling most of the time. Is this normal?

People never knew what I was going through, what I was thinking, how I felt, what I wanted, why I wanted it. Actually, did I even know all the answers to these???

Why are you so surprised that my mindset, thoughts, and attitude were so low, so damaged? Why am I so surprised that I felt like this? Ever since I was 5 years old, I had been in foster care with my sisters. I was making cups of tea and ironing. We had been in about ten foster homes in the space of three or four years. We had been abused with every type of abuse.

I had no guidance in my life or people I could trust. Everyone let me down. I did not trust anyone. Why should I? No one wanted me. No one believed anything I said or supported me when I was brave enough to speak out about what was happening to me. The adults that were meant to protect us didn't protect us like Sue/mum (or the foster carers in the homes we went into, as in many of them we were abused as well. I was the eldest out of three children. So, I felt like I was the protector of my two younger sisters right from the day they were born.

I can remember living in a family unit with Sue, her so-called partner, and my siblings. I was about three or four. I can remember the kitchen, the stairs, our one room apartment that had a wall separating the main living space, Sue's bed, and our room. It was high with a space at the top to the ceiling. We could hear everything. I can remember the horrible lady with curly hair that would say horrible things to us all. I think she was a mum living there, too. Sue's partner got into my bed one night and abused me. It was so awful. It felt like I was living in a nightmare... one that I couldn't wake up from.

I remember one day after coming back from the psychologist, sitting in the bathroom with Sue, with tall cream walls all around. She sat on the side of the bath, asking question after question about what happened and what I had said. The clinic had given me a crème egg, and I sat in the cream bathroom being questioned whilst the egg was melting, going through the wrapper and in-between my fingers.

It felt like soon after that we were all taken away from Sue. I can remember the day, going into the social worker's car. I was crying, hot, kicking and screaming swear words at them. If you are reading this now, feeling this way or remembering when you were taken away from your parents, think about whether it was the best thing for you or/and your siblings? I know it was for us. You can get through anything, be brave and strong.

I stayed with one sibling; the other went to another home. She was six months old. I missed her and always worried if she was OK.

I had a very troubled relationship with Sue/mum in my teens as I didn't really respect her for not protecting myself or my sisters when we were young. Isn't that what mums are supposed to do? I wasn't meant to be the one looking after my sisters, changing their nappies, feeding them, ensuring that men who came around to see my mum didn't come by them as these men were always drinking and on drugs.

Most children remember the good things in their younger childhood. But did I have any good times? When I was only about three or four years old, Sue was chased down the street with a knife... all I could do was run, screaming at the top of my lungs, "Leave my mum alone!"

Different men were in the house all the time. There are so many memories. Why can't I just block them out? You may have memories from when you lived with your parents, but remember to move forward. You should not have seen, heard, or experienced many of the things you did. Think about having some therapy/counselling to get through it, so it doesn't affect the rest of your life in different areas. It will affect you in areas you will not realise, so dealing with it now will help to build stronger relationships, find closure, and not have to deal with the hurt and lack of self-confidence, self-belief, and self-worth later in life.

By the age of eight, I was being left in the house with our young siblings when the foster mum went out. I couldn't play with them, just in my room with a piece of tissue lodged in the door, so when the door opened, it would fall, which would alert my foster mum I had been out of the room, though I was clever and put it back. Everyone needs to go to the toilet, don't they? That is a basic need. We couldn't keep holding it in for hours.

Sometimes, we weren't fed enough or even starved for up to three days. I was physically abused and hit with belts. Due to the abuse over all the years, I was still wetting the bed at this time. It was embarrassing, but I just could not control it at all. It was painful. I felt so lonely. I couldn't tell anyone; if I did, who would believe me? The foster mum would just keep lying like she always did anyway.

I was so sad all the time. If you are in the same position, please don't worry; the bedwetting will stop when you feel safe and comfortable with your surroundings. Also, when you stop worrying, the anxiety goes away or eases.

After years of abuse, I couldn't take it anymore. So, I decided to ask to be removed from that home. My sisters didn't want to come. I felt so guilty leaving them, knowing the abuse would carry on. Contact with my sisters after that didn't really happen as their foster carer would make up excuses not to bring them. I wrote letters to social workers all the time about what was happening to them but was told that unless they ask to be removed, there was nothing that could be done.

I didn't see Sue/mum for nine years, but coming back to Birmingham, she had to be informed. Social workers were asking if we wanted to see her. I didn't want to. Why would I? I had no love or respect for her for what she had done and not protecting us when we all needed her.

When I decided to see her, it was to get what I wanted from her. She allowed me to drink and smoke! When I drank, it would make me forget things that had happened, giving me time to get out of my own head and stop thinking. So why not use her?! She had never done anything for us before. So, I continued, for years, until I was an adult. My sisters had gone to live with her, but things were not good. I hated that Sue/mum had married the man that had got into my bed when I was younger. How could she do that? She chose a man over her children. We were taken from her, though instead of fighting for us, she stayed with a man that abused us! He was an alcoholic, and I hated my sisters being there. So much happened in those years.

Drinking was not the way out though. Now, I know of the dangers of drinking – what it does mentally as well as other bad effects on your body. It also makes you very vulnerable and unsafe as a person, and in different situations you may be in. As alcohol is a suppressant, it actually makes you feel worse and makes your mental health low so you don't feel happy. Overcoming the trauma that you have experienced is the best way forward. Addressing what and why things happened will help you to make better choices as you get older. If only I knew this when I was younger, my life would have been so different.

As a foster child growing up and as a teenager, I didn't feel heard or understood. Regardless of what the situation was, the foster carers had listened to or believed other people in that situation, and I was punished for it. Like if I was touched by a man, they didn't do anything about it. There were times they saw this happen and did nothing. They didn't believe me and always put it back on me, asking what that person would think if I went out there spreading these horrible rumours about them.

By this age, about 16, I had no trust in anyone. All the people that were supposed to have protected us didn't. Who did I have to speak to? Who would believe me? Why wasn't I understood or believed as a child? There are different charities and organisations that you can call if you are in these situations (see numbers at end of the chapter). Call the police and explain what is happening. It is not okay for these things to be happening to you or people you know. It has to stop.

People didn't know my experiences or what I had gone through. As a teenager, I didn't want to talk about it. I was offered counselling, and I didn't want counselling. Why should I go to counselling? I didn't believe counselling worked; why would I need to talk to people?

I wasn't understood as a teen at all. The most obvious was at school. I hated school and was bullied. I did not fit in anyway and hardly had any friends. Actually, I didn't think that I could even speak to anybody about how badly I hated school. I felt like I was in my own head a lot. If other teens in school found out about me being fostered, what would they think? Would that be another reason for them to bully me?

I didn't really talk about being a foster child or that I lived with foster parents. I wasn't able to stay out at people's houses, and there were certain things that I wasn't allowed to do because I was a foster child. How can you talk about that when other people had families and they had a mum or dad or both? The social workers support was very rare from what I can remember, and how could a foster parent support me when they hadn't been through this themselves?

This is only a very small part of what happened in my childhood/teens. I have a whole other book to write. So, in summary, being in foster care can cause a lot of pain, mixed feelings, anxiety, depression, not understanding yourself and why these things happen, or how it will affect us long-term.

It has taken me a long time to discover self-love and grow self-worth, self-confidence, and self-belief. There are loads of things you can do, including speaking to therapists and having healing work in different ways. You can journal about your feelings and write every day what you love about yourself. You can meditate and write things you are grateful for each day.

Don't let it take you until you get into your thirties or forties to learn or deal with what happened as a child, as you are GREAT! You are AMAZING! You are YOU. Do not let your childhood experiences and the people that have made it awful for you growing up define who you are. Do not get into drink and drugs to block your memories or because you think it helps. Find the self-love and self-care strategies to ensure you have self-worth. Surround yourself with people that lift and support you. Be a strong person who is brave, confident, strong. Find who you are and what you want to be and run with it. YOU have got this.

Shine, you beautiful star, shine the brightest. You have so much to give – so many gifts, experience and knowledge; go conquer the world. Do not let anything hold you back.

Love Jane

About Author

JANE MILLER

Jane Miller is a parent coach and entrepreneur. She is also a partner, mum to a 16-year-old and a fur mum.

Jane was a foster child for most of her childhood. She has experienced a lot through her life as a child and an adult. Life has definitely been challenging, and she has had ups and downs throughout it. Now, Jane is hoping for more ups with her passion about helping others, such as foster children. She knows what foster children go through and how to understand them and support them in the way they need. If you are ready to transform your life, become the best version of yourself, have self-belief, confidence, and self-worth, go shine now. Connect with Jane at http://www.facebook.com/JaneMillerParentCoach or https://www.instagram.com/_janemillerparentcoach_/

Chapter Nine

To the teen who loves their neurodiverse siblings

By Emily Jolliffe

To the teen who loves their neurodiverse siblings but doesn't always understand them,

I know it can be hard. Maybe your brother or sister isn't always kind to you or easy to understand. Perhaps they take up a lot of your parents' time, and you feel there's less time left for you. I acknowledge that it's likely harder for autistic people experiencing the world differently. The neurotypical social world maybe doesn't feel like their native language.

It's hard in different ways as a neurotypical person to relate to neurodiverse family members. You're trying to learn their language in what can feel at times like a hurricane, so we know that no one's finding it easy! No one is to blame, and no one makes it difficult. It's where we are. Blaming doesn't give us any solutions; we're all doing the best we can with what we know today. There's no hierarchy of who has it worst, no relative suffering, no family pecking order of pain.

Two of my four brothers are autistic, and I have two neurodiverse sons. My brothers were diagnosed in their 40s, so I didn't know they were autistic growing up. I don't even recall hearing the word "autistic," much less "neurodiverse," as a child and teenager in the '80s and '90s. It was touched on for a day and a half in my teacher training, which is more than the single mention my mum heard when she trained as a teacher in the '60s!

Any mixed feelings I had towards my brothers were simply as brothers, and we didn't know they had a diagnosis until decades later.

Looking back, earlier diagnoses would have been helpful for all of us – firstly for my brother who says he thought he was bad for being different. It would have been helpful for my parents to know how best to support him effectively and helpful for us siblings to understand better how they ticked, and support that more and earlier.

We live in a wonderful age when, fortunately, diagnoses of autism, ADHD, dyslexia, etc. have become much more common at younger ages; it's great news for families seeking to get help for their loved ones.

The terminology around neurodiversity is becoming less foreign, and people are more familiar with the words and concepts. Each April is Autism Acceptance Month; cinemas and supermarkets have autism-friendly shopping times and screenings. Things have come a long way, even in the last decade since my son was diagnosed.

There's still a way to go, however, in terms of inclusion and tailored support, especially for women and girls, who often mask their autism, covering it up to fit in and learning the language of a largely neurotypical world. Even in autistic spectrum assessment and diagnosis, the questions asked are based on the white male autistic experience, meaning many girls and women are undiagnosed and under-supported. This can be compounded by the trauma of struggling in silence and other mental health diagnoses like depression and anxiety that can result.

If you see your sister or friend with special interests struggling to interpret expressions or subtleties of conversation, how can you reach out to them? A kind word or even a sympathetic glance can help. They might be open to talking about it to you or a trusted adult. Suffering in silence is lonely.

As Hannah Gadsby, the comedian, says:
"It is difficult for women... there is a certain place on the spectrum that is reserved for the great white (male) geniuses, and they're allowed to hyper focus on their special interest and be terrible at interpersonal communications, and they're held up as... the best of men. It's much more difficult for women because of the expectations in the social network that we're supposed to uphold, and when we fail, that is a failure of character."

Neurodiverse girls, especially, can experience worry and anxiety around school, and tummy aches and missing school are common manifestations of this. Self-harm and eating issues are becoming more widespread following lockdowns, especially among neurodiverse teenage girls.

I look back and remember the possibly undiagnosed autistic girls at my school in the '90s, too – the ones who memorised whole comedy sketches, the quiet ones, the bookish ones, the ones whose repetitive self-soothing behaviours we sometimes thought odd at the time. I already see my children's generation being kinder to each other more often (in front of me anyway). I think they're braver at calling out bullying, less cowed by peer pressure. This doesn't just happen; it's a mass of tiny kind actions, like speaking inclusively, making space for others.

I see my three children navigate their relationships with each other on the good days and the trickier days. I don't believe, as many blithely declare, that, "We're all on the spectrum." I know many autistic people find that belittling of their experience. I love the response I've read by #ActuallyAutistic advocates: "Yeah, just like we're all a little bit pregnant!"

My own three children are neurodiverse and have issues with sensory processing, some harder to assess. One is noise sensitive. They think they're being told off if we speak firmly to their siblings. One can be really loud and energetic! One was diagnosed as autistic at age 7 and has a history of hurting others. This behaviour has since transformed, but it has been hard for siblings to forget.

Growing up, I knew my brother wanted to spend a lot of time alone and reading. He found out in his 40s, to his enormous relief, that he's autistic. If you feel different and find 'normal' social things harder than others seem to (like small talk – does anyone really love it?!), there can be important solidarity in knowing about and meeting others who are different in the same ways.

When my autistic son was being assessed, we explained by saying he was differently wired, as my autistic brother had shared with me. In other words, his brain worked differently. Different isn't wrong; it's just different. And there's room in the world for everyone to think differently.

No shame, no big deal; we wanted to be useful to him, as with all our children. We referred to others he knew who were also autistic, while bearing in mind the saying, "When you've met one autistic person, you've met one autistic person"! No one child or adult represents all autistic people.

It was helpful to us, his parents, as well as his siblings, to know that he thrived on 1-1 time and needed alone time to decompress and digest the stresses of interacting, what he saw as demands, or the sensory overload he felt from a trip to the shop.

We found ways to prioritise that 1-1 time and ensure he got alone time when needed. We made ourselves useful to him by entering into his world and deepened our connection by following and joining him in reading, playing, and chatting together – on his terms.

While one parent spent 1-1 time with him, the second parent would be with our other children. Over time, we trained other helpers to play with our boy, so he could experience a wider social variety, and we could spend more time with all of our children and working.

Small children frequently cry that, "it's not fair!" Their sense of justice is keenly honed. Parents mostly do their best to listen equally, to give according to the needs of each child. As a child, it may not seem fair to you, but short of cloning ourselves, parents will go where the need is. Just as we don't do the Heimlich manoeuver to all the children, only the one who's choking.

As a parent, I've seen my children become more kind and generous with others, especially others who are different. They've learned some brilliant lessons and are more compassionate humans. They might not have learned these lessons if they didn't have a neurodiverse sibling. I'm proud my children are developing these parts of themselves. Of course, if you do feel you're not getting enough time or attention, absolutely ask for what you want.

What would I say to my own teenage self? I'd say, "You'll learn more than you ever imagined about a subject you've never heard of!" I studied languages – French, Spanish, Russian, and Italian. All parents learn to speak "Child," even the special dialect of Child their own kid teaches them, while the adults slowly stumble through each lesson. We learned "Autistic Child" as well, our son's unique dialect. We and his siblings are still working out this dialect as we go, though we've become much more fluent, at last, now that our lives are in a calmer, more predictable stage. Things do get easier.

Just as the first step in learning to pronounce an Italian word is to listen to an Italian speak it, the first step in learning to communicate with an autistic sibling or friend is to listen to them. And listening sometimes requires all our senses. As with neurotypical interactions, what's unspoken matters too – tone, gestures, reading signs of comfort or discomfort. Can you be present and humble enough to let them be your guide?

I think what I learned from my brothers helped me work out my children's languages, though I didn't realise it at the time. My own parents showed love and acceptance to all five of us as different souls. They gave us a lot of space to be ourselves and prioritised happiness over achievement, which I'm very grateful for (though I didn't show it much as a teenager!)

Sibling relationships can be wonderful, and they can also be hard. We help rub each other's edges off, or sand them down at least! As children, we practice being ourselves on them before launching ourselves out into the world. We might complain bitterly to our friends about them as kids and teens. We know and remember each other's young selves, sometimes cringingly well. If we're lucky, siblings are there for us through life's challenges as well as the celebrations. I'm blessed with ones who have been there for me and my children.

Embrace your neurodiverse sibling! Having an accepting sister or brother can really help their strengths and confidence emerge. What are the things you enjoy about them – even if it's one simple thing you have in common, or laugh at together?

Neurodiverse people offer different ways of looking at the world and being in it. Neurotypicals can learn from them much-needed perspectives to the challenges of our time in history. How can you help your sibling or friend navigate the neurotypical world? What ways can you challenge a stereotype of neurodiverse people? One action, one day at a time.

What gift does your sibling bring that you can celebrate? Perhaps they're really good at being in the moment, are self-reflective, have a great memory, or let things go quickly. Let's look with the eyes to find their amazing qualities. You don't have to understand someone completely to love them. We seek to understand them more, and that is bound to be easier when we start with love and acceptance.

It wasn't always easy, but I've rewired my own brain to look for the gifts of neurodiversity while supporting the difficulties. This now helps me look for blessings and learnings every single day in other parts of my life.

Make sure you look after your own needs, too, including asking for help when you need it, from parents, teachers, neighbours, and others you trust. Everyone in the family needs support, not just the loudest or the one with the most obvious special educational needs.

Our families, communities, and our whole world benefit when we make space to welcome differences, whether our brains are neurodiverse or neurotypical, whether we start off speaking the same language or not. Our common humanity bridges all these differences. This bridge is built on all our little actions, including towards our siblings. They all add up to a kinder, more open and generous family and society to live in.

Love Emily

About Author

EMILY JOLLIFFE

Emily Jolliffe is a couples and 1-1 counsellor, specialising in supporting parents through tough times.

She offers tailored well-being/autism coaching and small group programmes on themes like setting boundaries with love and working with our children's motivations. She provides Zoom sessions to clients in the UK and internationally. She loves walk and talk sessions with those in the Bath/Frome area.

She's a certified counsellor in the Option Process Dialogue and an accredited coach with the Independent Authority for Professional Coaching and Mentoring.

Before retraining as a counsellor and coach, she worked in education and conflict resolution.

You can find more information at www.getclarity-letgo.co.uk join her group for parents of autistic children here www.facebook.com/groups/specialparentingtogether or connect at www.instagram.com/emilycounsellorautismcoach

Chapter Ten

To the teen who is struggling with self-worth

By Enjoymasuela Tjorn

To the teen who is struggling with self-worth and hiding their true self because of the fear of rejection,

Content warning: sexual abuse and attempted suicide

What people think about you is their issue, not yours! Their opinion is based on what THEY see (and often their issues), but they don't see the struggles you have had to endure.

What if I told you it is possible to rewrite the story of your life?

Do you know that what you believe will manifest?

You are greater than what others think.

When I was 10 years old, I was playful and carefree, but in an instant, in one cold moment, my childlike innocence turned into emotional distress. Indeed, one moment altered my entire teenage life.

On one lovely day, I was enjoying playing with other kids in the neighbourhood. That was one of the best moments... until the lady nearby turned on her black-and-white TV. So what can you expect kids to do? I stopped playing outside and went to watch it instead. I rushed into her house. I don't remember if we asked for permission, but it seemed okay with her to have kids in her house... except she seemed to have a problem with me in particular. As soon as she saw me, she immediately walked toward me, grabbed me by my arm, and took me outside.

What happened next created a ripple effect through my teen and adult life. I'll never forget what she said to me, "Who do you think you are? Don't you know you are the child of the split bamboo culm?" (an idiomatic expression commonly used in the Philippines when a child was born out of wedlock). "You have no right to come to my house. Look at your ugly face. Your eyes and teeth are big like a rabbit! Get out of my sight right now, and don't you ever try to come closer to my property again. You don't belong here!"

I was so frightened and felt humiliated. Immediately, I headed home and wept heavily. I internalised all the words she said. I grew up with my grandmother in a poor condition, and on top of it, I didn't know who my father was. Before that day, it never bothered me at all. However, some people felt it entitled them to be mean and cruel. If you let them, they will keep you from being true to yourself. I saw myself as a big mistake because I was born like this. I let her voice echo down to every fibre of my being on that day.

I have learned that once you permit others' beliefs, they slowly become yours. It deprives you of deciding for yourself. You become a prisoner of their opinion. And I know how it feels when you are confronted with those triggers. It happened to me during my time in secondary school.

I strived so hard to show up strong, defend myself, and please people in order to avoid rejection. It's such an awkward situation when you feel out of place. People dislike you. Living in a constant illusion of fear isn't an option but a way of life. Later, it becomes your reality, then your identity. And your belief about yourself becomes based upon it.

I felt envious every time I heard and saw my classmates go outside together with their dads. The most challenging event in our school was a "Father's Day" celebration. I literally hid in a bush away from the crowd until the program ended because I hated to see eyes on me, making me feel worse. This caused me to ask my mother about my father. It wasn't a pleasant conversation, but I soon had enough information to find him. Sometimes desperation finds the answer. And it teaches you how to persevere and never give up.

Counting the weeks until my high school graduation was an anxious time. Of course, emotions were running high, knowing that I was about to live independently alone in a big city. Stepping out into the unknown world was actually my biggest drive to keep going. It gave me a reason to look forward and gave me hope. It may sound peculiar, but it helped me a lot during this time.

The closer graduation got, the more enthusiastic I was about finding my father. It made my mission and obsession deeper. It also created curious questions like, "How does he look? How does it feel to be loved by him? What does his voice sound like?"

On the other hand, I was raised by a single mother who strived so much to make a living. She was committed to giving me a college degree. Finding a reasonable, cost-effective way of living was my gesture of supporting her. I lived in an unpleasant boarding house in a tiny room with no window and the stink of the canal filling the small room. I cut down my food budget, but not my tuition payments, so I could continue to study.

This new start made me more responsible and more mature – ready for new challenges. Being insecure makes life a challenge, and it is such an awful feeling to go through. That's why on most occasions at school, I was all alone. Although I made some friends on campus, I would rather be by myself.

I thought often about finding my dad, but I was waiting for the right time to do it. In the meantime, traveling back home by boat once in a while on the weekend was also quite a challenge. I got easily sickened by the waves. On one particular sail, a knight in shining armour came to the rescue. Who wouldn't give such regard to a random act of kindness?

In a short amount of time, we became friends. Even though he was much older than me, it was not an issue. After meeting a few times, our conversations became more intimate. It struck me when he made a promise to help find my dad.

I know how hard it is when you can't trust anyone. Therefore, trusting someone was a crucial decision for me. But I let down my guard and allowed him to touch my body parts, but the sexual intercourse it led to was against my will. This was the first time in my life and then it happened again and again until I realized he was just lying. He was manipulating the whole situation.

I felt so bad. I betrayed myself by breaking the promise to keep the most sacred/precious part of me for my future husband. Unfortunately, I gave it so easily to someone I didn't love. I was left with so much shame, guilt, hatred, anger, bitterness, and the list goes on.

When you begin to question your worth and value to yourself, it means your self-respect is also fading. You're probably trying to pretend that you are OK, but deep inside, you are all messed up, slowly dying while striving to do the right thing just to please your parents and friends.

I managed to keep my studies on track for my mom's sake but not my well-being. I dated several men as a sort of punishment, distracting myself from the ugly reality. It brought nothing but complete darkness. What do you do when your life is falling apart? The more you try to clean up your mess, the more miserable you get!

One day, as I was standing in front of a mirror, I saw an ugly demon face, and it scared me to death. This stopped me from using the mirror for months. My head faced down as I walked outside, and I made no eye contact with anyone. During my second year in college, I was seated in the last row and left our classroom without notice.

Some may say you get over it in time, but for me, it was the opposite. The longer it took, the more hopeless I got. My biggest dilemma was how would my mother react? What about my friends and other people who have their expectations of me? That was it! I reached my breaking point. I could no longer carry such everyday torture, and my conscience was eating me alive, not to mention the guilt, shame, condemnation, and unworthiness inside.

Ending my life was my last resort to stop the agony. In the middle of the night as the passenger boat I was on was sailing smoothly heading to my home island, I climbed up the railings at the backside area of the boat and was ready to jump. Fortunately, a man came and intervened. I guess it was not my time to die.

If you have done the same and survived, were you grateful or angry? What does that mean to you? What I believe it means is that God has not finished with you yet! I don't know if you believe in the Lord Jesus, but I do. When I was 14, I started knowing him. Honestly, it didn't keep me away from trouble, but surely, it does help me go through life.

I'll never forget a powerful experience on one special night. In a stinky, four square meter room with no window. I was desperately saying to God, "If you are a real God according to what I've read, to what I was taught, and to what I heard, then show yourself right now and save me from dying. But if you can't, I'll surely die!" I slept deeply afterward.

As I woke up the next morning, my room looked like a paradise filled with rainbows everywhere. And for the first time, after months of not looking in the mirror, I saw my face with a glow from heaven and beaming with delight. I felt an overwhelming love of God all over me that brought new hope for a good change

That miracle was my turning point when I started to embrace optimism in myself. It opened a new opportunity to rewrite the story of my life. But does it take away all the emotional consequences of the things I've done wrong? Of course not!

There is no shortcut to mending a broken vessel. You really have to go through it. You really need to forgive yourself. You need to own your mistakes and not blame others for them. You need to choose to forgive those who hurt you, learn to let go, and learn to love yourself. Then, trust that the process will bring out the best in you.

Our failures and mistakes are the best teachers we have in life. Do not despise your small beginnings because they will journey with you toward your destination. The beginning may not happen how you'd hoped, but it always ends how it's supposed to.

Today, I'm enjoying the journey of loving, accepting, and knowing myself like never before. I hope my story inspires you to never give up, no matter what life brings to you. Remember that light is always at the end of the tunnel. This journey has taught me to see beauty from ashes. Although I may not be where I want to be today, I'm not where I used to be.

Thank you for reading my teen story.

Love Enjoy Masuela, at age 46

P.S. I guess you are wondering if I found my father, aren't you? I did try two times, but that was not the right time. However, in 2010 (I was 34 years old back then), I did meet him for the first time, and I'm guessing, my last time.

About Author

ENJOYMASUELA TJORN

Enjoy is a visionary woman by definition, an encourager, and a risk-taker who believes that all things are possible if you make them happen. During her depression and anxiety that lasted for years, she experienced living a life without life. It made her focus on helping women with mental illness by bravely sharing her story and providing practical strategies for emotional support through her short courses.

She is passionate about empowering women to connect with their true selves, so they can be the best version of themselves through self-love, forgiveness, and acceptance and so they can find their God-given purpose and impact the world. "Life is beautiful" is her motto because she can now see the beauty from the ashes.

She is a wife and a mom to two adorable boys who passionately love the Lord Jesus Christ. She is a native Filipino and currently living in Norway.

If you want live in a purposeful life and impact the world, then head on over to her website at https://enjoytjorn.com/ and grab her free resources or connect with her at https://www.instagram-.com/enjoymasuelatjorn/

Chapter Eleven

To the teen who feels trapped

By Eloise Grobbelaar

To the teen who feels trapped in emotional turmoil, feeling worthless and unsure of a happy future,

I know what it's like to feel alone, frightened, with nowhere to go, and desperate to feel safe and unconditionally loved - that was how I felt as a teen. That helplessness was very real then, but today, I can write to you, to let you know there is HOPE. You CAN do this. You can go and live a life that impacts the world around you, a life filled with love and laughter.

This letter is not about following my advice because you don't need me to tell you what to do. But I would like to take the opportunity to shift your focus and give you an opportunity to explore the possibilities. And the best way to start is to tell you who I am now.

At the age of 45 (yes, I'm that old!), I still don't have life sorted but I do have a much better understanding of what's happening, and because of that, I can be so much more purposeful in how I live. I have also not achieved everything I'd like to achieve but I am very proud of myself. I've led large community efforts, started a business, studied to get post-graduate qualifications, and trained over a thousand school staff and parents. I'm passionate about what I do because of my past.

I still haven't managed to move all fear and uncertainty out of my life, but I've learnt that taking big and brave steps means that I'm often out of my comfort zone. I've learned that it's possible to take big steps, whilst still weighing up the pros and cons so that those big steps are worth it. And in doing this I have become a stronger, more resilient person, more than I ever expected! I am also more confident in my own skin, most of the time, and I have found unconditional love in a safe and happy place. I married an amazing man, and we work hard at providing our kids with a lot of love, certainty, and safety, nurturing their personalities, and giving them space to grow.

And it's important to remember I am only human, I make mistakes more often than I'd like to, but I always try to do better and learn from the mistakes I've made.

At the age of 15, I was an awkward child, slight in build with very low self-esteem. And life then looked very different to what it is now. Here's some context through a bit of Q and A.

Q.   Did I have life sorted?
A.   No, I was a mess. I didn't have the skills or understanding to determine which bits of craziness and nastiness were inside me and which bits were poured over me. In my home, love was conditional, mixed with large amounts of shame and blame and used to manipulate my siblings and me. There was a lot of drama, so much of the time. Life was a rollercoaster with slight highs,

scary, deep dips, and tight, sharp turns. I couldn't predict just how often or how intense the tantrums would be, but I could be certain the next one was coming. These full-scale eruptions would vary between verbal (emotional) abuse and physical aggression. And so, even as a young child, I became very skilled at two things - walking on eggshells and being extremely perceptive to emotional cues. This was necessary for self-preservation. It was about at the age of 15 that I became aware that this emotionally charged reality of mine was not at all the same experience my friends had in their homes.

Q. Did I achieve much at that time in my life?

A.   No. I struggled with friendships. I had low self-esteem and always felt uncertain of how to handle myself. I tried very hard to fit in, which, of course, meant I didn't. I was a good athlete but would often self-sabotage events so that I didn't disappoint/upset anyone or myself. Academically, I achieved well below my abilities, getting low grades and scraping past. I didn't believe there would be much in my future, so I didn't see the point of trying to do better.

Q. Did I manage the fear and uncertainty in my life?

A.   No, I couldn't even label exactly what those feelings were. At around the age of 17, I believed that I only had two options - be bullied or stand up to the bully. I stood up, which meant that the fighting increased, the stress increased and I was told never to come near my family again on more than one occasion. I wanted to be loved and accepted so badly, that I looked for someone/anyone to give me that love and acceptance. I experienced bouts of depression, hiding in my room and dorm room so that I didn't have to see anyone and pretend to be happy. I actively made choices to engage in self-destructive behaviours, often feeling like I was on the verge of just throwing everything in the wind.

Q. Was I a strong person?

A.   I think I've answered that one, but just in case you missed it, no. I didn't think I'd be able to break free from the drama and craziness and most certainly did not think that I'd amount to anything. But at the same time, there was this urge to find my voice, to feel like I had worth. I wanted information before believing something. I wanted to voice opinions. I wanted to become my own person!

Q. Was I confident in my own skin?

A.   Again, no, I looked at myself as someone who could never be _____ enough. Whatever that descriptive word would be - clever, pretty, attractive, normal, funny, cool, interesting, confident, etc.

Q. Did I make mistakes?

A.   Yes, big ones, some of which had a direct and negative impact on my family for which I'm very sorry, and certainly, all the mistakes directly impacted who I became. I do not regret those decisions, they were absolutely necessary to get out of that situation. It was so intense, that with the insight and skills I had, I was left with very few options at that point. I am so very thankful for the grace I've experienced despite those mistakes and only wish someone was able to give me a glimmer of hope earlier in my life.

Right now, you might be reading this in the very thick of it, in the middle of a never-ending storm, and I want to encourage you and give you that glimmer of hope. You are a good person, nearly old enough to look after yourself and most definitely able to decide what kind of a life you want for yourself. You can make decisions and learn from the consequences.

Probably the biggest truth I learned was that my parents' issues did not have to become my issues (in my head, I have much stronger words to express that sentence). Through the way I grew up, I believed many lies. Have you spotted them?

~~Not good enough?~~ Lie!
~~Don't deserve unconditional love?~~ Lie!
~~Won't amount to much?~~ Lie!
~~Not able to break away from the craziness?~~ Lie!

Most importantly, I did not have to repeat their mistakes in my life, my marriage or with my own children. It could stop with me, now. This is where I started to make the shifts:

Shift no. 1: I can step out of their reality, look at it and decide what I want for myself.

I have always loved making lists. It's how I process information, how I make sense of everything and how I focus my attention, so naturally, as a teenager, I also made lists of what I wanted and what I certainly didn't want in my life. My list of "No thanks!" included the constant drama, the manipulative games, aggression, lies, hypocrisy, being bullied and often feeling afraid and worried. My list of "Yes please!" will come as no surprise as I'm sure this is what you want for your life as well.

- Unconditional love
- Safety (physical and emotional)
- Truth and honesty
- Calm
- Joy
- Adventure and fun
- A space to talk about my feelings

Shift no. 2: I can make sense of my past.

I knew that my parents had it tough growing up; they experienced abuse themselves. This was not an excuse, but to an extent, it did help me to make sense of my own childhood. Knowing what I know now about the importance of good mental health, I can also say that both parents struggled a lot. Between the two of them, there was a good mix of low self-esteem, depression, and more serious but undiagnosed and untreated disorders.

I can also look back at the decisions I made - the good ones and the bad ones - and reflect on why I made those. This brings me to shift no. 3.

Shift no. 3: I am responsible for my own actions.

This is a wonderful thing! I can actively work toward improving my own mental health. I can develop my emotional intelligence so that I become smarter with my decisions and responses in order for my life to have better outcomes. I want to have strong self-esteem so that even when I get things wrong, I can admit to it and show empathy and grace to myself. Strong self-esteem will help me to do the same for others, without allowing them to take advantage of me.

I don't want to be that bitter woman who blames everything on others and repeats those same mistakes with her own children. I want to be able to decide what's important and the steps I need to take towards achieving that.

I did say I wasn't going to give you any advice but (sigh ...), I wasn't able to stop myself. Just allow me this one piece of advice: Get off their rollercoaster. When you have people in your family who suffer from mental health issues, it's difficult to not get pulled into their drama. With all the growing I've done, I still don't think I'm mature and "grown-up" enough to actually ride their wild rollercoasters with them. And with certain disorders, if untreated, that rollercoaster will keep the same abusive patterns.

I have learned not to get on that ride. I've learned to protect myself, my marriage, and my children, by building strong boundaries and engaging with these family members on my terms. So here it is, my one and only piece of advice: You are important, you are allowed to be safe, you are allowed to set the boundaries and say "No". Get off their rollercoaster.

The truth of the matter is that life is like a rollercoaster. We know we can't control everything and can't predict everything. But we can have enough love, happiness, and trust in the mix so that when we do hit a tight turn or a big dip, there is enough to hold on to! If you address the hurt you have experienced, instead of getting dressed in the hurt, you can discard it and step away from it.

So go make those plans and go live that life ahead of you with the confidence that their issues do not need to be your issues.

Love Eloise

About Author

ELOISE GROBBELAAR

Eloise is a mum and a teacher with a specific focus on emotional intelligence, autism, and different behaviour approaches. She is also a certified parent educator, Team Teach tutor, Relax Kids coach, and has a post-graduate certificate in autism and challenging behaviour. She has had the opportunity to attend training by world-renowned Carol Dweck (in growth mindset) and Dr. Ross Greene (collaborative problem solving).

During the past 20 years, she has worked with various children with different needs. She is fascinated by the latest neuroscience research and the implications this has for our perceptions, approaches, and strategies when working with neuro-diverse children. This forms the basis of her teaching, whether in class with her students or teaching parents and professionals in a workshop. She also applies this in her own parenting! She enjoys empowering professionals, parents, and children with proven skills and tools to go beyond behaviour management and move instead towards raising happy, confident, and resilient children! Visit her website http://www.growthandgrit.org and connect with her on http://www.instagram.com/growth_and_grit

Chapter Twelve

To the teen whose parents divorced

By Faye Hancock

TO THE TEEN WHO feels they need to hold it all together whilst their parents divorce,

Time stopped on that journey home. It was less than a 2-hour drive, but when I think back, it felt like five. On one hand, I could see how unhappy Mum was, and I understood their decision, but at the same time, it felt as though I was one of those cartoons who had just had a building dropped on them. I felt crushed. What was going to happen now? Would our family ever be able to be together in the same room again, or was it all going to be arguments now? My head was spinning, and my thoughts felt like treacle. How was this happening to me?

Overall, I had a happy childhood. Despite asking when we were going to put my little sister in the dustbin when she wouldn't stop crying as a baby, I eventually grew to like her. We enjoyed playing games together, riding our bikes with the kids next door, and sometimes making up plays or home movies during school holidays.

My parents were young compared to my friends' parents; they had married when they were just 18 and 19, and I genuinely thought they were made for each other. They were inseparable, and to me, my parents could do no wrong. I loved them, they loved me, and they loved each other.

Divorce was something that happened to other people's families or celebrities who had been married for two weeks. It would never happen to my parents. Perhaps this was an underlying fear, a bit like the fear of a loved one becoming sick. You know it is possible, even likely, as we all get sick... but you never want to accept that it could actually happen to you.

I was 15 when I found out my dad had been unfaithful. It was incredibly painful to hear. I think I cried solidly for about three days. What made this harder to bear was that Dad didn't know I knew. Mum had told me in confidence because I told her I knew something wasn't right between them and wanted to know what was up.

Trying to process this betrayal, which felt like a personal betrayal against me and my sister, and attempting to forgive Dad for what he had done was the hardest thing I've ever had to do. No 15-year-old should have to bear such a weight.

On their 22nd wedding anniversary, our parents had a blessing in the same church where they were married. We all got dressed up, and it was a wonderful celebration. Standing there, with a beaming smile and a warm feeling in my heart, I was relieved and proud that they were both willing to work at their marriage and put things behind them.

But at this time, I kept diaries where almost all the entries were dark, depressive, and angry. I was hurting, and I needed an outlet for my pain. Writing about how you're feeling or recounting things that have happened to you is a healthy way of processing, and I encourage you to do so, but what is also helpful and can seem a scary thing to do is to talk to someone. Counselling at 15/16 didn't even cross my mind as I thought I was fine. My parents had patched things up, and I threw myself headfirst into my schoolwork, achieving straight A/A* grades in my GCSEs.

An opportunity for a fresh start came when I was making choices for university, and having lived in the same town for nearly 15 years, I was eager to find a place to create my own life free from the sting of betrayal and hurt. I couldn't wait to explore a new town and create fresh memories with new people. I moved to Bournemouth in September 2012, and I barely looked back. I joined a vibrant church, where I made friends my own age and shared many beach BBQs and late night chats with them. It was a brand new beginning.

For the whole first term at university, I didn't visit home once. I told myself this was a method of coping with the change and would help me adjust, and it did – I missed my family, but they came to visit. When my Mum came to pick me up and take me home for the Christmas holidays, I remember her face was gaunt, and the sparkle behind her eyes had vanished. She told me on the way home how things had become strained between her and Dad. She told me they had made the decision to divorce.

Time stopped on that journey home, and I felt crushed.

As my adult life was beginning, my parents' marriage was ending.

I'd known things were tough for a few months, but I hoped they'd work it out again. Christmas that year was hard. The house felt different – dull and quiet. This was a stark contrast to my new life in Bournemouth. Dad was distant. Mum was sad. My sister was lonely. I felt like I had to hold it all together.

All I wanted was a Christmas like all the others I could remember – Dad joking around at dinner and then falling asleep on the sofa, Mum playing the same Christmas CD over and over, maybe a family board game or two. But things had changed. I was so desperate to return to uni in January and leave it all behind.

It didn't take long for me to realise I couldn't leave it behind. Every day, the first thing that popped into my head was "Mum and Dad are getting divorced." It was like I couldn't quite believe it. It was like the foundations of my life were rocked to the very core.

It would be years until I labelled it correctly as a loss and began to properly process how it affected me, but my grieving started straight away. I drank too much. When I went out with friends, I became a liability, pushing myself to drink more and more until I was sick. I'm so grateful they took care of me and got me home safely. They were always there for me, listened to me, hugged me, ate ice cream with me. Friends are great, and the best friends will listen to you and support you through good times and bad.

But friends are not counsellors or trained therapists. Over the next two years, I relied on my friends a little too much. I couldn't see it at the time, as I was depressed, grieving, and experiencing feelings I'd never encountered before. My lowest point came in January 2015 during my final year at university, when two of my closest friends who I lived with sat me down and told me they thought I needed professional help.

Now, it needs to be said that they didn't do this sensitively, and my depressed brain heard them say, "We don't want you around anymore; we can't be there for you." Their words weren't exactly this, but they were very similar, and for me, this was a huge rejection. On top of everything I was processing and still going through, whilst figuring out what to do after graduation and worrying about my university work, my two best friends had turned their backs on me. I felt so alone. In the moments after this conversation, my heart was pounding, my chest was tight, I wanted to throw up. What now?

A year before this, I'd had a few free therapy sessions offered at the university. Something my counsellor said to me during one of our sessions still stays in my mind today – she told me that her driveway had flooded during a heavy week of rain, but that morning, she'd seen some snowdrops sprouting beneath the water. She told me I was like the snowdrops, blossoming even amidst the pressure and weight of it all. It was such a beautiful image.

But I didn't fully open up, and I was hiding how low I was really feeling, still trying to hold it all together. Clearly, my friends could see how low I was. They were worried about me, and that's why they tried to encourage me to seek help elsewhere – help they couldn't give me. That night, when my friends sat me down, my dad drove down to see me. We went for a drive, and he listened to me talk. The next day, I got up and went into my studio. Something in me reminded me of those snowdrops, and it gave me hope.

The next six months were a blur of course work. Again, I threw myself into my artwork, this time channelling all the emotion I'd been feeling, creating a sculpture that embodied that darkness and heaviness I felt. Anxiety became a daily part of my life. I needed to call my mum daily for several weeks just for her to talk to me to get me out the house. But as the weeks went on, I was feeling lighter.

I never got to a point of asking for medication for my depression, not that I was ashamed to do so, but because I'd had an awful experience with some medication when I was younger and was nervous after that. If you need medication to help with your mental health, that is totally OK. For me, it was God who pulled me out of my depression. He brought people around me who encouraged me; he reminded me of things I enjoyed, and day after day, his love for me kept me going.

Graduating with a 2:1 in July was a monumental achievement for me. I could easily have dropped out of uni. To have made it to the end, despite everything else going on around me, felt like a double success. I felt on top of the world that day – and to top it off, both my parents and my sister were there to see me graduate.

The following years were not plain sailing. My parents both remarried, and I gained several step-siblings. This was another enormous change.

I stayed in Bournemouth after graduating; it really was my hometown by now, and my church family was exactly that – a family. I did a voluntary year at church immediately after finishing university, and this gave me some time to just have fun and make new friends in Bournemouth as a lot of my university friends moved away.

My mental health dipped a bit in 2016 when this year ended and I needed to find myself a job to support myself and enable me to stay in the place I called home. I desperately didn't want to move back "home."

Fast forward to 2022, and I am happily married to my best friend whom I met through joining a choir in 2017. What I know now as a married 29-year-old is that marriage takes work. How could I have known that as a child?

I started having regular therapy sessions in 2021, and this has been one of the best decisions I've ever made. Finding someone you trust to talk to makes all the difference, and when big things happen and you have big feelings to process, often, the best person to talk to is a professional counsellor. Was it scary the first time I met my counsellor? Yes. Did I worry about what I'd talk about or how painful it would be? You bet. But has it helped me to process my parents' divorce healthily without impacting my friendships? Absolutely.

You don't need to hold it all together all the time. It's okay to admit that some things are too heavy to carry, that some feelings are confusing. It's okay to ask for help and to find someone to talk to.

These days, we like things to happen instantly. We crave a meal – a delivery person can have it to your door within minutes. We want to watch a specific film – the internet has thousands available at our fingertips. But some things aren't meant to be that quick. Processing, and the healing that comes from it, takes time. It's okay to be in that process. Sometimes, it will feel painful; other times, it will feel like a release. Allow yourself to be a work in progress.

You'll look back in 10 years like I did and see just how far you've come.

Love Faye

About Author

Faye Hancock

Faye Hancock is an artist, jewellery maker, and aspiring author. She is also a wife and follower of Christ and lives in sunny Bournemouth with her husband, Tom, whom she met at a local pop and soul choir. Faye is passionate about seeing people realise their potential, overcome barriers to personal growth, and conquer mental health issues. This is Faye's first published piece of writing, and she hopes to inspire others through sharing her story.

Visit her website https://www.fayebowdenart.com follow Faye on http://www.instagram.com/indigobearcreations to see her artwork and jewellery creations.

Chapter Thirteen

To the teen who is being bullied

By Kalini Kent

To the teen who is being bullied,

I stood rigid as the police officer delivered the result I had been dreading – that all these months, my secret tormentors were indeed my supposed best friends at school. A multitude of feelings surfaced, nearly making me sick – betrayal, shame, isolation, and feeling utterly let down, alone, and friendless. I didn't know who I could turn to. I wished I could just run away and end the pain of it all.

I wondered how it had all gotten this far and where it had all started...

I was born in the Caribbean, Guyana, the youngest of six children; we moved to live in Barbados when I was 2 years old, then arrived in London when I was 4.

From the moment I arrived, I felt different from everyone around me. It was a culture I knew nothing about, and I was petrified at how strange everything was.

I also looked different, dressed differently, sounded different, and, as a result, was treated differently at school. Here is where the taunts and jibes started, just for being different and not understanding how things ran.

As an example, a girl in my class went to Brownies (which I knew nothing about), and her surname was 'Brown,' so I thought that was the criteria for getting in. No one enlightened me.

Looking back now, my time at primary school was traumatic. Teased for many things, including innocent things like my middle name being Florence, I grew up not understanding a lot and not fitting in because of cultural differences. We never had other kids around our house to play or for tea, as I was so embarrassed because what we ate was different. As a result, I was incredibly shy and socially isolated with only a few people I could classify as "friends," but none that I could speak to and share things with. In those days, my definition of a friend was someone who didn't tease or ostracise me.

So a bit like "Mr. Cellophane" in the musical Chicago, not wanting to rock the boat or draw attention to myself, I kept quiet often and tried to be invisible. I felt like I didn't have a voice.

The impact of all this was great. For a shy and impressionable child, it made me so insecure, fragile, and lacking in confidence, constantly worrying and anxious and looking for the next incident or episode.

Secondary school was equally difficult, and memories of my teenage years were of loneliness and anxiety. I moved to an all-girls school, but no one from my primary school went, so I knew no one, and it was a frightening experience. I found it difficult making new friends, mostly because everyone else seemed to know each other, and once again, I felt like I did not fit in.

Feeling alone and friendless, it was difficult finding that one bonding friendship that would give me security. This seems to be a regular thing with friendship groups at school – especially with girls – that constant shifting and changing of friends.

There were several instances of break-ups and make-ups, of people talking behind your back, and multiple forms of bullying, including taunts, social exclusion, and being made fun of.

I just didn't understand it. Why did people have to behave that way and be so nasty? My own values were such that I would only treat people how I would like to be treated myself. So my expectation was that others would be good, kind, and honest, but unfortunately, you know that is not the case.

We all seek that one person we can trust, our ally whom we can turn to and depend on, who gives us some level of security, someone to go around with, and who gives us that status in social terms of being liked and worthy. But not socialising with anyone out of school made it hard to break down barriers and forge the friendships we were seeking.

Unfortunately, it was only once I was in my GCSE years that I really found strong friendships with two girls who really helped me to feel safe and believe in my worth.

Prior to that, I found myself in the all-too-common scenario of chasing friendships and never feeling "enough." Instead of staying true to myself and believing that I was worthy of being liked and wanted, I unfortunately got involved in a very fickle group of girls who proved to be my nemeses.

It started with occasional anonymous phone calls, with maybe one or two people talking in disguised voices. The content was always explicit sexual content and very disturbing. I was so distraught that I would go to school the following day upset and withdrawn.

It was affecting me in so many ways, to the point of feeling quite ill with the stress of it all. I was so embarrassed and felt trapped, as I felt like I could not share it with anyone. I never even mentioned it to my parents.

Eventually, I broke down and told one girl at school, not realising that she was the one doing it.

Then came the fake concern and interest shown about what other calls I had received. So the calls became more frequent and even more graphic, with me reporting back to them at school what was being said. Little did I know they were taking delight in the growing distress they were causing.

Nowadays, this would be the equivalent of cyberbullying of the worst kind, and it had been going on for some months.

My parents only finally found out once they overheard one call and then took it into their own hands and involved the police — something I had always feared. But it was the only way, as things had become serious.

Finally, one evening, the police traced one call and recorded it, and I discovered my persecutors were the group of girls that I had thought were my friends.

The moment of finding this out was terrible and filled me with so many emotions.

Why would they do it?

How could they be so unkind to make me feel like this?

I went into school the following day feeling utterly alone, friendless, and ashamed. But I was also frightened in case they had told everyone about it, and I would be a laughing stock. I also feared I would face repercussions because the police had been involved.

The worst of it was that I did nothing. I said nothing and never told the teachers, mostly out of shame and the embarrassment of saying what had been happening. Plus, fearing repercussions, I just took it on the chin and internalised it. I even said "hello" to my tormentors as if nothing had happened.

This was like them getting away with it, but I chose the course of least resistance as I just needed peace and for things to stop. Things did die down as the police arriving on their doorstep had frightened them. But I had a secret win as I did not let them know how much it had affected me. Looking back now, what I realised was that they knew that I knew and that was enough. I could walk away from them with my head held high.

Whilst this entire episode had a marked impact on me, I realised it made me a much stronger person. Yes, it left me sometimes overly concerned with how others viewed me and sometimes wary. But that is not a bad thing, as we need to maintain healthy boundaries in life.

The main thing that I achieved, though, was the realisation of how resilient I am.

Looking back, my entire childhood was a troubled and turbulent time. But I learned many things and grew so much as a person. I realised that the group of girls that I had made important in my life were, in fact, not good for me and I did not need them.

I also learned that we cannot choose what happens to us, but we can choose how to respond. That is something we have control over, and we have choices. Our past trauma does not need to define us. Instead, we can choose to love ourselves and shine, face our fears, and carve the future we want.

What happened helped me decide to focus on the things that I could do well rather than focusing on the things that were wrong. I knew I was good at sports and drama, and these were the two things that eventually helped me become the independent and confident person I am today.

Others noticed my sporting ability, which helped build my self-esteem and self-worth. Through joining a hockey club and tennis club, I was doing things that gave me joy and joining new friendship groups.

I also loved performing arts. This was surprising, really, as I had been shy and lacking in confidence. But it was escapism and allowed me to be who I wanted to be without the labels and stereotyping I had lived with. As a result, I became a lot more confident and able to communicate effectively, and it helped me to find my voice to speak up and speak out. It also drove me on to support others to find their voices and resulted in what I do now.

Whatever you are feeling right now, I want you to know that those feelings are valid. But we must always remember that we have so much to offer the world and that things will get better. Life may seem tough right now, and it may sometimes be difficult to see the light at the end of the tunnel, but we should know and believe that it will get better.

There are things that we can do to help ourselves, and these are some of the things I have learned along the way that I hope will help:

1.   Find ways to boost our confidence and self-esteem, and develop a belief in ourselves and our abilities so that we have unshakeable confidence.

2.   Try to find ways of strengthening our resilience muscles so that we can bounce back from setbacks and manage the challenges life throws at us.

3.   Develop a growth mindset so that instead of focusing on problems, we are always seeking the possibilities that exist.

4.   Try to adopt a positive mental attitude to life so that we are not overcome by negativity and the attitudes or behaviour of others.

5.   Surround ourselves with supportive people who love and care for us, even if it is just one trusted person whom we know we can turn to and believes in us.

6.   Find the things that interest us, we enjoy, or that we are good at – perhaps a new hobby – which will give us access to like-minded people and will help build confidence in our own skills and abilities.

So wherever you are in your journey right now, above all, my message to my younger self is to remember H.O.P.E. – Hold On, Pain Ends. You are enough, and you are loved.

Love Kalini – your older self xx

About Author

KALINI KENT

Kalini is a communication and drama specialist, and works as a youth, parent, and family coach, helping young people develop the skills to thrive, realise their potential, and achieve their aspirations, whilst supporting parents with the many challenges they face.

She is passionate about all forms of communication, and uses confidence, resilience, and mindset coaching to help people develop the skills to confidently communicate and present effectively, find their own unique "voice," and overcome any fears and doubts standing in the way of success. This is particularly the case with young people. Her 30+ years as a theatre director, staging award-winning productions, has helped countless children gain confidence to speak up and speak out, build resilience, and be who they want to be.

She works extensively in schools delivering workshops on the programmes she has written including her anti-bullying programme - 'AB360,' plus 'JIGSAW Youth Life-skills, Employability and Wellbeing.' Both programmes give young people the strategies they need to manage life's challenges and become the best versions of themselves. Being an ACES (adverse childhood experiences) trainer and mental health first aider, trauma and bullying have become a major focus of Kalini's work with young people and adults.

Visit her website www.kalinikent.com and connect with her via the links here https://linktr.ee/KentK

Further Support

If you are struggling right now and need further support please speak to a medical professional.

Here are some organisations that can help:

Young Minds: Mental Health Support For Young People | YoungMinds (www.youngminds.org.uk)

Childline: Childline | Childline (www.childline.org.uk)

We Mind and Kelly Matters: We Mind & Kelly Matters (wemind-andkellymatters.org.uk)

Acknowledgments

Wow, what a journey this book collaboration has been!

I am thankful to all the authors for trusting me with their stories and being part of this amazing adventure! To see the authors open up and use their letter writing as a way to help process past experiences has been an real privilege. Their enthusiasm to want to make a positive impact on future generations is awesome and I am thankful to have partnered with them through *Letters to my Teenage Self*.

Thank you to my family and friends for all their support in this process and to God for sustaining me through the hard times.

Thank you to Meggan and Martha for their coaching and wonderful support in running this collaboration, they both helped me believe I could actually do it! Thank you to Sophie for providing training in epistolary writing, proofreading and her ongoing encouragement throughout this process. Thank you to Meggan for writing the foreword, Holly for designing the cover and Melissa for editing.

Thank you reader for taking the time to read *Letters to my Teenage Self*, I hope that it has inspired you and helped you know that you are not alone in your struggles.